THE GAY MARRIAGE ALTERNATIVE

Finding Legal Equality, Security, and Peace of Mind Without Changing the Law

Jeffrey G. Marsocci, Esq.

Domestic Partner Publishing, LLC

Note regarding legal counsel

As with any product, it is important to be clear about its intended purpose and use to avoid any misunderstandings. Specifically with writings about legal issues, it is noted that these materials are not a substitute for competent legal counsel. The contents of this book are instead written to provide information about partner protection planning solutions available to domestic partners in an era where gay marriage is largely banned in the United States. The contents of this book are not to be construed as legal advice, and no attorney-client privilege exists between the reader and the author and/or publisher. In addition, laws change frequently, and therefore you also are urged to speak with an attorney about changes in the law that may affect you.

Circular 230 Disclosure: To ensure compliance with requirements imposed by the Internal Revenue Service, unless specifically indicated otherwise, any tax advice contained in this book (including any accompanying literature) was not intended or written to be used, and cannot be used, for the purpose of avoiding tax-related penalties or promoting, marketing, or recommending to another party any tax-related matter addressed herein. For specific legal advice, you are urged to contact an attorney in your state or jurisdiction.

About the Author

Jeffrey G. Marsocci was born in Fort Worth, Texas, and raised in Lincoln, Rhode Island, where he graduated from Mount Saint Charles Academy High School. He received his Bachelor's degree in Business from Hofstra University, and two years later earned his law degree from the same university.

In 2004, he received a Certificate Degree in Non-Profit Management from Duke University, and has earned his Legal Master of Estate Preservation designation from the *Abts Institute for Estate Preservation.* Jeff also serves as a member of the Legal Council for The Estate Plan™, a nationally recognized estate preservation company headed by Henry Abts, trust guru and author of *The Living Trust.*

Jeff has led his own firm in Raleigh, North Carolina, since 1996, focusing on the areas of Wills, Trusts and Life & Estate Planning with a concentration in assisting domestic partners and other unmarried couples. He is also a founding member of The National Institute for Domestic Partner Estate Planning, and he frequently participates in programs to educate attorneys, financial advisors and accountants on estate planning issues.

Jeff and his wife Kathleen are active Kiwanis members, working with the college-based service organization Circle K throughout North Carolina and South Carolina. Jeff and Kathy also each received the President's Call to Service Award for performing more than 4,000 hours of service during their lifetimes.

This book is dedicated to all those who find a way, no matter what.

TABLE OF CONTENTS

Introduction

A gay couple walks into a restaurant, hearing it was a great place to eat. Before the waiter can take their order, the manager walks over and asks if they are a couple. A little taken aback, they both reply, "yes." The manager becomes clearly upset and asks the couple to leave, saying "We don't serve gay people here."

The couple gets up and storms out of the restaurant, yelling about how discriminatory the restaurant is. Outside, the couple talks and begins to get more and more upset at the way they were treated. They start yelling and screaming at the restaurant through the door. They then go to a nearby hardware store and make signs to protest the restaurant and start their own picket line, encouraging people to boycott the restaurant until they agree to serve everyone.

They stay outside the restaurant all night and all of the next day, vowing to keep up their protest 24 hours a day, seven days a week. The manager comes out at one point and tells them that no matter how much they yell and scream, they will not be served. This goes on for five days, each day the manager coming into work ignoring the protesting couple and ignoring them just as much when he leaves. On the sixth day the manager comes in to open the restaurant and finds the couple dead at the front door.

They had starved to death, never having gotten anything to eat.

There is injustice and inequality in the world and it deserves to be confronted. But it should not be confronted while ignoring other methods of getting what is actually needed. While it seems ridiculous that the gay couple in the story would not find something to eat at some point in their six days of protesting, this is precisely what hundreds of thousands of committed domestic partner couples do when they protest anti-gay marriage laws but ignore the tools right in front of them that can protect their partner and their future together.

Despite state constitutional amendments and despite inequitable marriage laws, domestic partners have the tools they need to get even more protections and rights than signing a marriage certificate ever could. Revocable Living Trusts, Domestic Partnership Property Agreements, Powers of Attorney, and other legally binding partner planning documents are available to domestic partners *right now in all fifty states.*

No waiting. No watered down rights. No bowing to an electorate.

"That's fantastic!" you might say. "Great news! Where do I get in line!?" Then you may say, "wait a minute… why haven't I heard of this before?"

There are several reasons. First, the truth is that television and talk-radio news media make money on controversy. A lot of money. And aside from political sex scandals, there is nothing that boosts ratings (and advertising dollars) more than the controversy over gay marriage. So why would the media take the high but less lucrative road of avoiding the controversy and simply giving the good news? They won't.

Second, while the solutions to helping domestic partners meet their goals have been there all along, there are a lot of attorneys, accountants, and financial advisors who shy away from concentrating on legal partner protection planning because they feel it may jeopardize their relationships with other clients. Being in the "Deep South," or nearly so, I can understand the fear, but wholeheartedly disagree with it. Since writing my first book *Estate Planning for Domestic Partners: The Legal Secrets You Need to Know to Protect Your Partner and Your Future*, there are very few clients who have stopped using my services, and those who have gone away were problem clients I didn't necessarily enjoy working with in the first place.

There are also a few attorneys who focus on helping domestic partners, but they have set up their shops trying to be "anything and everything legal" to their clients, handling Will drafting, adoptions, discrimination lawsuits, and even traffic tickets for their LGBT clients. As a result, most of these attorneys have become legal jacks of all trades and masters of none and have not concentrated on fully developing the concepts, applications and legal solutions necessary to give their clients everything they could under the law in the specific area of legal partner planning.

Finally, there are probably some larger firms who may have developed some or all of the solutions we will discuss in this book, but they have not moved to promoting the solutions for the general public. My speculated belief is that if they have these solutions, the larger firms are probably charging a few of their wealthier domestic partner clients tens of thousands of dollars for the solutions, making it difficult for the average couple to afford. As a result, word wouldn't get around very well.

These are the main reasons most domestic partner couples have not heard of these legally available solutions. But there are solutions to helping domestic partners gain most of the rights married couples take for granted and then some. I did provide a detailed explanation of these solutions in *Estate Planning for Domestic Partners*, but I felt a shorter book giving the solutions without the examples and the explanations would be highly beneficial, and so *The Gay Marriage Alternative* was conceived.

In addition to providing an outline of the solutions, there are also other resources available to help domestic partners gain these marriage-equivalent rights through personal planning. The Estate Plan™ is a national document production and education company that has The Domestic Partner AB-SECURE Trust™ available to attorneys in all 50 states. No matter what state the partners are in, an attorney can contact The Estate Plan™, become an affiliate, and then have this trust available to their clients. (www.theestateplan.com).

Because legal domestic partner planning is a highly focused field where mistakes are common and can be costly, advanced training for attorneys, financial advisors and accountants are available through The National Institute for Domestic Partner Estate Planning. All members of the Institute have gone through basic life and estate planning education, have attended advanced domestic partner planning training through the Institute's programs, and have become members of the National Ethics Bureau or have had similar professional and legal background checks. If you need a professional to help you get the process started, then The National Institute for Domestic Partner Estate Planning is a good place to start. (www.NIDPestateplanning.com).

As you can see, there is hope for domestic partners in gaining most of the equal legal rights (if not the equal legal recognition) they deserve without changing the laws to allow gay marriage. In the face of two consecutive federal election cycles yielding state constitutional amendments banning gay marriage and brining the total states banning gay marriage to about 30 and the number of states passing laws banning gay marriage to 40, it could be decades before national gay marriage is a reality. Domestic partners shouldn't have to wait, nor do they need to anymore.

Chapter One: Gay Marriage is Beside the Point

Gerry and Dean were partners for many years, and they were completely committed to each other. They desperately wanted to protect each other, but were greatly concerned about the upheaval over gay marriage. Early in the new millennium, they watched gay marriage in Hawaii with keen interest, and were greatly discouraged when it was taken away. Suddenly, the Massachusetts residents were elated to find their own state's constitution was ruled to mandate gay marriage! They were among the first gay couples to get married in Massachusetts in 2004, and finally, finally, Gerry rested easy knowing that his retirement would be transferred to Dean should anything happen to him. After all, Dean was now his spouse.

In 2007, Gerry passed on, Dean tried to apply to receive Gerry's pension and was flatly denied. They refused to recognize the marriage as valid for purposes of Gerry's pension, and the legal system agreed. Dean was left without the support a spouse usually gets, and certainly without the support Gerry and Dean thought they would get with marriage.

Unfortunately, this is based on a true story. Gerry is Gerry Studds, a former Congressman from Massachusetts, and when Gerry died his partner (and under Massachusetts law, his husband) Dean Hara was unable to receive Gerry's government pension. "But they were covered when they got married… weren't they?"

Domestic partners have traditionally been at a distinct legal disadvantage compared to married couples. Hundreds of years of legal precedence, statutes and cases have been compiled, automatically giving couples special rights and privileges upon marriage. The common belief is that until same-gender couples are legally allowed to marry, they will never gain the advantages and rights marriage confers... and when they can marry, they will have everything they ever wanted. The reality is that marriage is not all that it is cracked up to be.

Before going into what rights marriage confers, let's first take a look at typical domestic partner goals. While each situation is different, most domestic partners have the following goals:

1) bring everything together as one family unit

2) allow partners to make medical and financial decisions for each other in time of sickness or after death

3) allow partners to inherit from each other

Most domestic partners wish to combine their assets so that they can act as one family unit. If either partner owns an account, their partner can take money out, or, for a brokerage account, change the make up of the investments. If one partner owns a home, then their partner should be able to sign off on home repairs or sign for delivery of new furniture just as if they owned the home themselves. In its simplest terms, partners want their assets to be share and share alike so "what's yours is mine and what's mine is yours."

Domestic partners generally trust each other, have faith in their partner's desire to act in their best interest, and understand what they want. In that spirit, they want their partner to be able to make legal and financial decisions on their behalf, whether they have fallen ill or not, and they want their partner to take over their healthcare decisions should they not be able to. More importantly for some, they also do not want their "closest" relatives to make decisions for them to the exclusion of their partner and *their* feelings.

Finally, committed partners make a promise to foster and protect one another. They live together, build their assets together, and when one of them passes on, they want their partner to be as financially secure as possible by inheriting everything that they own. After all, in both a real and emotional sense, they helped build all of their assets and so they should be entitled to them if one partner passes on.

These are the main rights that most people, including married couples, associate with marriage. People assume that with a marriage certificate comes an automatic merging of assets and resources. People assume that a marriage license is a license for a person to sign any document and make any decision for their spouse. People assume that because they are married in the eyes of the law that their spouse gets everything.

These people are wrong.

Marriage does confer some rights, but some of those rights are only partial in nature. As society has "progressed" and divorce becomes more and more prevalent, people are rarely being allowed to make financial or legal decisions for their spouse without some sort of written permission or without the spouse actually being judged legally incapacitated by a court. While possession isn't really nine-tenths of the law, you can imagine someone planning to divorce their spouse emptying all of their spouse's separate bank accounts in addition to the joint accounts. Getting the money back becomes a nightmare, and you better believe that banks have been sued for not protecting a person's separate accounts from a divorcing spouse.

While people are investing in stocks, bonds, and other devices, most people still list their home as their greatest asset. Mortgage companies are not going to give a pile of money to one person based on the value of a home jointly-owned with their spouse and simply let that person sign for their spouse. Cable companies, telephone companies, and other service providers have also started ignoring requests from people to make changes to accounts in the sole name of their spouse. When you really look at it, legally and practically, marriage is not all it's cracked up to be.

Probably the biggest surprise to married couples is that many states do not have 100% inheritance by a spouse. (Pause. Wait for expressions of shock.). Yes, that's right, just because someone is married does not mean they will inherit everything from their spouse. (Yes, many married couples are wandering around in a legal fog, ignorantly assuming everything they want will magically happen if disaster strikes.) For example, in my own state of North Carolina, the only time a spouse inherits everything is if the deceased person has no children or descendants living and no parents or grandparents living. If they had one child when they passed on, then they get about half and the spouse gets the rest. If there are two or more children, then the kids split about two thirds and the spouse gets the rest. If there are no children, but at least one parent alive, then the parent gets half and the spouse gets the rest.

At the time of publication, the only states that have gay marriage are Massachusetts, Connecticut, Vermont and Iowa. Surely, these states will provide partners with the inheritance rights they are looking for… right?

Wrong. The Massachusetts rules are actually worse. A survivor is only entitled to half of their spouse's property over $200,000 if the deceased spouse has any of the following still living—a child, a parent, a niece or nephew, a sibling, a grandparent, or a cousin—not just a parent or child. Even if you and your partner are married, living in Massachusetts, and have not done any legal estate planning, the survivor may end up splitting an inheritance in half with a third cousin that neither of you has ever met. In Connecticut, the rules are similar, and Iowa the spouse first gets all of the real estate before dividing all of the investments and bank accounts with the children. So unless a deceased partner has absolutely no living relatives (or they actually put together a written and legally binding estate plan), the partner will be splitting the assets with *someone*.

For many domestic partners interested in protecting their partner and their future together, obtaining gay marriage may still be an honorable and justified goal, but it is not going to give their partnership exactly what they want. It's like the gay couple finally winning their fight with the manager of the restaurant and being served, only to find that the food wasn't all that good to begin with. It's time for domestic partners to find *real* solutions that can give them *everything* they want. But as we will see in the next chapter, there are some supposed "solutions" that do little more than create a legal mess, a financial mess, or both.

Chapter Two:
Folk Remedies That Do Not Work

Debbie and Barbara were together for 20 years, and they prided themselves on taking care of all of the little details. Debbie was a successful architect, Barbara kept their home and their small arts and crafts business going, and both of them made sure all of their records were complete and accurate to a fault. They even had a commitment ceremony three years into their relationship. But a few years ago, they took additional steps based on advice they received from some friends. They placed Debbie's house into joint property with a right of survivorship with Barbara, drafted Wills through the attorney who handled a speeding ticket for Debbie, and set up a system of depositing money into Barbara's account to handle the household expenses. After talking with their friends and seeing what they did, they were sure they were covered.

Now, 3 years later, Barbara is sitting in the lawyer's office crying. It has been 8 months since Debbie died and she is still unable to get to any of the accounts because they are all going through the probate court system. The house was all Barbara's, but the mortgage payments were a few months in arrears and there was a threat of foreclosure. The other bills were falling behind, and now her part-time business that was more of a hobby is now a full time necessity to put food on the table. Further, Debbie's brother is contesting the Will, dragging out the proceedings and making life difficult for Barbara. Now, the last straw that brought Barbara's world crashing down, the IRS was auditing the estate and is questioning why no gift tax forms were filed in the 20 years of their relationship when it seems clear that Debbie had been transferring cash to Barbara. The truth that Barbara needed the money to buy food and other items for the house has fallen on deaf ears.

"What did we do wrong?" Barbara asked her attorney.

Sometimes conventional wisdom is not so wise, and it takes more than advice from a friend to handle things the right way. Unfortunately, a lot of layperson advice gets followed and, in the area of legal partner protection planning, the problems are not realized until years later. In this chapter, we will review three of the most common life and estate planning mistakes and explain why they are mistakes. (For more information on other planning mistakes frequently made by domestic partners, please download the free report *Five Common Pitfalls in Domestic Partner Estate Planning That Can Cost Thousands of Dollars* at www.domesticpartnerpitfalls.com.)

Specifically, we will look at:

1) Wills
2) Joint Property
3) Beneficiary Designations

Planning Mistake #1: Using Wills

Probably the most popular document for estate planning is the Last Will and Testament. All adults can spell out their wishes for what happens to their property after they pass on. As long as the format complies with state law and all debts and taxes are taken care of, their property goes to the people chosen. Of course, there are some exceptions in state laws, such as a wife not being able to completely cut out her husband, but by and large property goes to the designated beneficiaries.

A Last Will and Testament can name executors to handle the details of moving your estate through the bureaucratic probate court process, nominate guardians to care for minors, and appoint trustees to manage the inheritance for underage beneficiaries and accounting the courts. It can also designate beneficiaries, create age and other restrictions and provide specific instructions for handling certain property.

For domestic partners, drafting wills that name each other as beneficiaries may seem like the correct course of action to protect each other. After all, this is what most married couples also do. It is extremely important to note that using a will has some serious drawbacks regardless of your marital situation. First, using a will guarantees your assets go through the probate court bureaucracy before being distributed to your chosen beneficiaries, which means high settlement costs, time delays and a higher possibility of your plans being contested.

Probate is the legal process of transferring title of assets from a deceased person's name to the names of the rightful beneficiaries and heirs. In the most basic terms, probate is a re-titling process. But in order for a court to be assured there is no embezzlement or corruption before transferring those assets, many inventories, appraisals and other tasks have to be completed, documented and reviewed before the court will finally let things go. It is this process, which was originally designed with good intentions, that causes such extreme drawbacks for partners.

The amount of money spent on the probate court process may shock you. There have been numerous studies over the years. While there is considerable variance in the costs associated with probate, I feel comfortable estimating that probate eats up between four and ten percent (4 percent-10 percent) of an estate's assets. Nationally, that's about $4 billion annually, and growing.

For example, let's say Andy and Barney have not done any life and estate planning except for having wills drawn up. Andy passes away, leaving Barney a condominium that includes furniture and appliances, a stock portfolio, and various other assets totaling $500,000. The rough estimate of probate costs would be between $20,000 and $50,000. There are some law firms that will actually charge a flat rate of five percent of the total value of the estate to handle all matters in settling the estate, so Andy's estate would cost $25,000 to settle.

I can hear probate attorneys mumbling about how that's ridiculous, and how the probate court fees are nowhere nearly that high. They're right. Probate *court* fees are not that high, but their argument is just like the life insurance salespeople make when they say there are no taxes on life insurance proceeds when there actually are estate taxes but no income taxes. The reality is that probate *court* fees are not the issue. What is at issue are all of the attorney fees, appraisals, paperwork and related expenses necessary to complete the probate process. In North Carolina, probate court fees are 40 cents for every $1,000 and are capped at $6,000 in fees. (See the North Carolina General Statutes Chapter 28A). Next time an attorney tells you probate is not that big of a deal and the probate court fees are low, be sure to ask him or her if that includes all of the other filing fees, appraisals and attorney fees as well, and if he or she would put it in writing.

Now, I want to be clear in criticizing some of my fellow attorneys. I have no problem with probate attorneys who take on difficult-to-settle estates. They put a lot time and effort into their work, and it is not their fault the probate court has stringent requirements they have to meet. It is quite probable they deserve every penny of the 4-10 percent they charge. My problem is with estate planning attorneys who tell their clients *during the planning phase* that they don't need to avoid probate for their estates, or that probate is no big deal. These attorneys are either not knowledgeable in avoiding probate, or, much worse, they know exactly what they are doing and are counting on huge legal fees in the future for probating the inexpensive wills they draft now.

It also takes a significant amount of time to probate an estate. Settlement times vary even more greatly than costs, and there are some states with special, more rapid procedures for small estates. However, anywhere between six months and two years is a likely estimate for most estates, and that does not include those estates where the will is contested. Much of this is time is wasted on trips to the courthouse or to the attorney's office, time spent gathering information in order to fill out detailed inventory and report forms, and time spent with your life in a holding pattern while all of the formalities of probate are observed. Even worse, particularly for domestic partner couples, the deceased's accounts may be tied up during probate, leaving the other partner financially handicapped.

Wills are also much more susceptible to challenges than other methods of legal planning, such a revocable living trust. (www.theestateplan.com). For domestic partners, protecting against challenges from the angry relatives who want to cause trouble may be the primary motivation for even addressing life and estate planning. Attorneys who suggest a Last Will and Testament and nothing more may be unknowingly setting their clients up for a legal or financial fall.

The reason wills are easier to contest is because a will is formed at one point in time. The most frequent method of contesting a will is claiming the deceased was not "in their right mind" when he or she signed it. All that is needed to cast doubt on the will signing is behavior around the one point in time. Let's say a person saw a psychologist the week before he signed his will. An upset beneficiary may start yelling and screaming "See! He was crazy to cut me out and leave everything to his live-in friend!" The one appointment combined with an emotional plea may be enough to move a judge to at least examine the state of mind of the will signer around the signing date.

This is not the case with a revocable living trust because it is not acted upon only once and not again until death like a will. If someone wanted to prove a person's revocable living trust is invalid because the person was not in her right mind, then someone would have to cast doubt on her actions each and every time she acted with the trust. For example, if Alice's brother doesn't like the fact she is leaving all of her assets to her partner Vera and he wanted to show she was not in her right mind, he would have to show that was the case: 1) when Alice signed the trust, 2) when she transferred a savings account into the trust, 3) when she refinanced the house owned by the trust, 4) when she named the trust as a beneficiary on her life insurance, and 5) every other time she acted as a trustee or beneficiary of the trust. This can be stretched to also include every time she wrote a check from an account owned by her trust.

In particular, attorneys have to be extremely careful in recommending wills for domestic partners because of the comparatively high number of relatives willing to make trouble over an estate. It is probably much safer to establish a revocable living trust and properly fund it for no other reason than to help deter challenges in the future.

While these three reasons—high settlement costs, delay and contestability—are all valid points to recommend using a revocable living trust to avoid probate, there are many more reasons to use a revocable living trust. In fact, an entire book has been written on this subject. For the foremost non-legal text on revocable living trusts, please read *The Living Trust* by Henry Abts III from McGraw-Hill.

By now, you hopefully have the right impression that probate is something to be avoided. Unless there is no one you trust to take care of your last wishes and you refuse to appoint a trust company, then there is no need for the probate court to be involved. There are a few ways to avoid probate, but some carry their own risks and costs. Of course, I'm referring to joint property and beneficiary designations.

Planning Mistake #2: Using Joint Property

Whenever two people commit themselves to each other, they invariably get around to discussing how their home is titled. If one person owns the home, the person wants the partner to feel he or she has equal ownership in the house. So the natural urge is to re-title the house in both partners' names with a right of survivorship. Simple? Yes. Effective? *No.*

What joint property fails to account for is the federal gift tax that allows only the first $13,000 (in the year this book was published) given from one person to another without the tax being imposed. Every dollar after that is subject to a gift tax. However, the federal government, in all of its renowned mercy, graciously allows $1 million to be gifted over the course of your life without you actually having to pay the tax. The downside is it also lowers the amount dollar-for-dollar you are allowed to pass on without estate taxes upon death.

Before we get to an example, and before you tune out completely because of the million dollar exemption, the real danger here is not the actual payment of tax, but the failure to file a gift tax form with the IRS. Because of two of the IRS's favorite words "interest" and "penalties," it is best to stay above board on all of these transactions. The other reason for reading on and keeping gifts to less than $13,000 a year is to avoid having to recreate records when the IRS audits a person's estate and finds multiple gifts without a gift tax form being filled out. If you record all transactions properly and avoid situations where gifts of $12,000 or more per year are made between partners, then you can prevent huge accounting bills in the event of IRS action. (For more information on gift and other taxes affecting domestic partners, please download the audio interview with Bette Wagner, CPA available at www.gaymarriagealternative.com).

Please note this is only related to federal gift taxes. Until recently, my home state of North Carolina imposed a gift tax on every dollar above $12,000 gifted between domestic partners in a given year. For more information on how the gift tax may affect you in your own state, please see a qualified accountant or CPA in your area for specific tax advice.

Now, for the example:

Andy and Barney are partners, and they decide to live in Barney's home. Instead of talking to a legal partner planning attorney, Barney talks to his brother's mechanic's sister-in-law who used to work as a real estate loan processor, and who tells Barney to just do a deed saying Andy and Barney own the house as joint tenants with a right of survivorship. Depending on the real estate attorney Barney gets to handle the deed, he or she may not even know or care about gift taxes. Barney's house and land are worth $400,000, so half of it is a gift from Barney to Andy.

Looking at the numbers, the $200,000 gift was made from Barney to Andy. The first $13,000 is exempt in that year, so provided Barney does not make any more taxable gifts to Andy, there is a gift of $187,000 to be reported. If this is the first time Barney has to report any taxable gifts in excess of $13,000, then we can deduct the $187,000 from Barney's lifetime gift exemptions of $1 million, and $723,000 remains that Barney can still gift during his life. You also have to deduct the $187,000 from the $1 million Barney can pass to others without estate taxes when he dies (post-2011). That leaves $723,000 Barney can leave to others estate tax free when he passes on.

The procedure for Barney to report these gifts is to fill out a federal gift tax form, currently Form 709, as well as any gift tax forms his state requires. He should also keep a running total of all gifts given so he does not unintentionally give more than $1 million in taxable gifts during his life and would then have to lay out cash to pay the gift tax. The gift tax does not only apply to land, but everything else of value as well, such as stock and other accounts.

Another drawback to joint property with a right of survivorship is it only looks one step ahead. When one partner passes on, the other will receive the property, but what happens if both partners pass on together or within a short amount of time of each other? The property will have to go through probate before it can be distributed to the intended beneficiaries. Good legal partner planning looks more than one step ahead to cover multiple contingencies and avoid probate for all of them. With the right revocable living trust, the property can be titled in the name of the trust, all of these contingencies can be spelled out, and the property will go where it was intended without probate.

Let's use an example to cure the referenced drawbacks of joint property. Rather than use joint property with a right of survivorship, Barney and Andy decide to create a joint revocable living trust with an integrated separate property agreement (which may be a Domestic Partner AB-SECURE™ Trust). Andy places the house into the trust and lists it as separate property belonging to him.

Now the house is owned by the trust, both Andy and Barney are equal trustees and owners of the trust, but the domestic partnership property agreement keeps the property technically separate for gift tax purposes. It is also listed that the house will go to Barney if Andy passes on, and if Barney passes on first then it will go to his nephew Greg. If Greg passes on, it will go to his cousin Peter. If Peter also passes on, it will go to his friend Bobby. And if Bobby passes on, it will go equally to his sisters Marcia, Jan and Cindy. Now the property not only avoids the gift tax problems associated with joint property, but it now lists multiple levels of beneficiaries who would receive the property upon death without the property having to go through probate.

Planning Mistake #3: Beneficiary Designations

In an effort to make things simple and avoid probate on accounts and life insurance, many institutions allow their clients to name beneficiaries on the accounts, and many even allow a place to indicate a contingent beneficiary. While this is good for the client, it is also good for the company because now it is not in the middle of a probate proceeding that may be contested. Legally, the company is fulfilling its obligation after the death of the client once it transfers the account to the new named owner. In most cases, and depending on the company, it is a quick process taking a few days to handle the paperwork and make the transfer. (For more information on life insurance, please see the audio interviews with financial advisor Jessica Lamb, and financial advisors Bobbie Hilburn and Michael DiPenta available at www.gaymarriagealternative.com).

While beneficiary designations are not as lethal to some plans as wills and joint property with a right of survivorship, there are still some drawbacks to using beneficiary designations rather than a revocable living trust. As mentioned before with joint property, it only accounts for one transfer upon the death of the owner. If and when the owner passes on, it will go to the person or persons listed as the beneficiary. What if that person passes on before them? Financial institutions which allow for contingent beneficiaries have let the client take care of the first "what if" by listing a contingent beneficiary, but what if this beneficiary passes on as well?

By using a revocable living trust, all of the different contingencies can be listed within the trust, and now the account is handled properly, without probate, regardless of how many years pass by and how many different people may have passed on. Depending on the type of account, the account can either be placed into the trust directly or the beneficiary designation features on the account can name the trust as the beneficiary upon death. Now the account can stay in the individual partner's name during life and name the trust as beneficiary upon death.

There is another serious drawback to using beneficiary designations, and the best way to illustrate this is through an example and a simple question.

Alice and Vera have a son, Tommy, who is 18. Alice and Vera each have managed to accumulate assets. Aside from the family home, their biggest assets are two brokerage accounts worth $500,000 each. One belongs to Alice and the other belongs to Vera, so Alice lists Vera as her primary beneficiary on the account and Vera lists Alice. Both list their son Tommy as contingent beneficiary. Vera and Alice are involved in a car accident and both pass on. Tommy will now receive their brokerage accounts, without probate. Now for the question—what do you think 18 year-old Tommy is going to do with the $1 million?

Most parents understand that while they love their children and they may be legal adults at 18, most 18 year olds are not responsible enough to effectively handle a large inheritance. By placing a child's name on a beneficiary designation, the child gets control of the account at age 18, should anything happen to the parent. If instead, a revocable living trust was listed as the beneficiary, a trustee would manage this account for Tommy's benefit until he reaches a more suitable age. Alice and Vera could plan ahead by naming a succession of trustees to handle things and choose the age of distribution, such as when Tommy turns 25 or 30 years of age.

We have now covered three of the biggest legal planning mistakes, as well as the reasons why they are mistakes. But you have also seen there is hope for successful planning. The main method for avoiding the problems outlined here is covered in the chapter devoted to The Domestic Partner AB-SECURE Trust™. In many situations, it is exactly what domestic partners need as the core of their legal partner planning. For more details on avoiding domestic partner legal planning mistakes, please download the free report at www.domesticpartnerpitfalls.com.

Chapter Three:
The Domestic Partner AB-SECURE Trust™

Two years ago, I was reviewing a lease agreement for a client's new restaurant and my receptionist buzzed through, asking if I had a minute to talk with someone on the phone about his mother-in-law's estate. She mentioned that he was referred by another attorney we knew who handled real estate closings, so I told her I would take the call.

His frustration was immediate. As he spoke, it was clear he didn't even want to make the call, but his wife was making him. The main thing was his wife was sure her mother had a life insurance policy, and 'a long time ago' she was told by her mother that she was the beneficiary. "I can't find out anything about her estate, and it's just not right what's going on."

I asked a few more questions about where he checked for information. They called the clerk of courts office and was told that the executor had been appointed but there was no other information on the assets. They checked a few insurance companies the wife remembered seeing bills for a long time ago to see if there was a policy, and they were told they could not give out that information to anyone but the executor.

"Well, something doesn't sound quite right," I told him. "Who is the executor?"

He paused for a minute, as if trying to figure out whether or not to tell me something, and he said, "That woman who calls herself her partner *is the executor, and I tell you it just ain't right that her daughter can't get information."*

As he explained how it shouldn't matter that they barely spoke in the last five years and that no matter what that woman called herself, she was not family, I was starting to see where this was going. Nonetheless, I wanted to make sure of the legal situation, even though I had already decided not to take the case. I asked, "If her estate is going through probate, then the asset list is publicly available. Are you sure her estate is in probate, meaning she used a Will to handle distributing her assets?"

I heard some papers shuffling in the background. "The lady at the court told me that her property was in some kind of… wait a minute and let me look… yeah, a revocable living trust. What the hell is that?"

I then went on to explain that a revocable living trust avoids the probate court system, is private, and if it were anything like the trusts we draft and his mother-in-law's partner was the trustee, then there was probably very little he could do. He then politely thanked me for my time and hung up while mumbling "it just ain't right."

Now that we have examined typical domestic partner goals, a failure of marriage in general to address those goals, and looked at folk remedies that don't work, it is now time to discuss some solid solutions that can help domestic partners reach their goals. If done correctly, a joint revocable living trust can form the core of a private and secure domestic partner plan and be the main vehicle for avoiding many problems faced by couples in general and by domestic partners in particular. When people ask what a trust is, I tell them "In the simplest terms, a trust is a legal entity that you and your partner create during life that can combine your assets, give each other complete control, and provide for the smoothest possible transition if one partner passes on."

Finding the right attorney

Some attorneys are familiar with revocable living trusts as a means of avoiding probate for their individual and married clients, but there are not a lot of attorneys who know how to successfully create a trust for domestic partners. Worse still, there are many attorneys who think they know what they are doing when it comes to legal planning in general, but in truth they only have a cursory knowledge and assume because they passed the bar exam, they know everything.

Unlike other areas of law, it is difficult for an attorney to know if he or she messed up until it is too late. If a real estate deal is messed up, chances are someone will catch it. If an attorney messes up procedure in a divorce, the opposing attorney, clerk or judge will point it out. Unless another attorney proficient in life and estate planning reviews your documents, there is usually no one else in the process who would know what was wrong until the documents were needed. *And once a person is deceased or incapacitated, there is little, if anything, that can be done.*

It is always a good to sit down with an attorney and ask questions before hiring one. In order to help you find the right attorney and other professionals in putting together your legal partner planning, you and your partner should look for the following warning signs:

- They recommend using joint property with a right of survivorship and never mention gift taxes.
- They tell you all you need are Wills and you don't need to discuss a trust.
- They say probate is not a big deal and their firm handles probate cases all of the time.

If you notice any of the above points, then they clearly do not have the knowledge to help you and your partner with legal partner planning. This is not to say they are bad lawyers, but I've often seen lawyers who are very good with real estate matters, or family law, or traffic court cases want to help when their clients come to them with another matter like drafting life and estate planning documents. The problem is they don't realize it is not that simple.

While there are a lot of lawyers not able to truly handle legal partner planning for same-sex couples, there are also some attorneys who understand the concepts and who are doing a good job of protecting their clients and addressing their needs. But they are still not doing the *best* job they could. It's the extra care, thoroughness and using the right documents that can give domestic partners 100 percent of all possible protection versus the 80 percent of the most important protections. Here are three typical signs your attorney may be doing a good job but not the best job possible:

- They insist on drafting separate revocable trusts because of gift tax problems with having a joint trust.
- They acknowledge there are some estate tax problems but tell you only married couples can double-up their estate tax credits.

- There is no way to transfer more than $13,000 between you in any given year, so if you want to equalize your assets, one of you should just write a check for $13,000 to the other each year

Here the attorneys are showing they understand estate and gift tax implications for domestic partners, which is big step ahead of some attorneys, and they may be able to do a good job putting together a legal plan for you and your partner. But it also indicates they don't have some of the advanced knowledge to give you all of the protection, tax credits and joining assets together the law allows. With the right documents and language, you and your partner can combine most of your assets in a single revocable living trust. With the right revocable living trust, you and your partner can double your estate tax credits. And with the creative use of corporate entities and other techniques, it is possible to move much more than $13,000 worth of property from one partner to the other.

Finding a professional who knows how to give domestic partners the best of all possible legal partner planning worlds is as simple as finding them through The National Institute for Domestic Partner Estate Planning (www.NIDPestateplanning.com). The best documents are also easy to find since they are offered through The Estate Plan™ (www.theestateplan.com). The fact I am available to consult with these professionals on domestic partner issues and they would most likely be using the documents my firm helped develop with The Estate Plan™ means domestic partners have an easy way to start their search.

Putting together your legal partner plan should not have to be a hit-or-miss proposition, and it all starts by working with the right attorney and other professionals. To download the free report *The Five Critical Questions to Ask About Partner Planning*, go to the Resources Section of www.gaymarriagealternative.com.

Highlights of the joint revocable living trust

Because of the volume of books on the market which review the benefits of using a revocable living trust rather than a Will, we will only cover the main points here. This book is more appropriately focused on applying all of the legal planning documents correctly to domestic partnerships. And if you start with the Partner AB-SECURE™ Trust from The Estate Plan™, then all of the positive features are already incorporated into the trust. For a more detailed general description of the benefits of using a revocable living trust versus a will, I recommend reading *The Living Trust* by Henry W. Abts III.

For purposes of this chapter and domestic partnerships, the following are the main advantages of using the right revocable living trust:

1) Most property can be combined into one trust for the two of you so you are acting as one family unit.

2) Distributions upon death are all handled according to the terms of the trust, with all of the "what ifs" and contingencies in place.

3) All assets in the trust before death and those transferring into the trust automatically after death do not have to go through probate. Because the assets do not have to go through probate:

    a. settlement costs are lower

    b. settlement times are much quicker

    c. the settlement process is private.

4) The revocable living trust is much harder to contest than a last will and testament.

Again, like attorneys, all trusts are not created equal. To make sure you are getting the best documents available at an affordable price, we recommend you contact a financial advisor or attorney affiliated with The Estate Plan™ for a Partner AB-SECURE™ Trust (www.theestateplan.com). To find the best possible professionals available to help with these documents, you may want to search for a professional through The National Institute for Domestic Partner Estate Planning (www.NIDPestateplanning.com) and ask if he or she works with The Estate Plan™.

Acting as one family unit

In setting up your joint revocable living trust, you and your partner are taking on three roles—trustors, trustees and beneficiaries. As trustors, you are the people establishing the trust. As trustees, you are both jointly empowered to utilize the trust assets for the benefit of the beneficiaries. As the beneficiaries, you are the people who enjoy the trust assets. Together you and your partner are taking control over all of the assets in the trust, together you are both running the trust for your best interests, and together you are benefiting from the trust.

In terms of owning everything together, a joint revocable living trust is as close to dual ownership as domestic partners can get without violating gift tax rules. Partners can now act upon each others' assets as if they were their own. The only difference is they are technically doing so as a trustee.

Distributions upon death

Taking into account the inheritance portion of legal partner planning, domestic partners naturally want to provide for each other when one of them passes on, but what happens when the second partner passes on? There may be children or not. There may be favorite nieces and nephews, friends or siblings. How is property divided?

All of the distribution wishes for both partners are included in the revocable living trust, listing all of the contingencies. Most domestic partner couples chose one of four main plans to start with, and then make some subtle changes. The plans are:

1. When one partner passes on, everything goes to the surviving partner outright and when he or she passes on, everything goes to beneficiaries jointly determined by both partners.

2. When one partner passes on, everything goes to the surviving partner outright and when he or she passes on, everything goes to the beneficiaries of the second partner.

3. When one partner passes on, everything is accessible to the surviving partner, and when he or she passes on, all of the first partner's separate property and one half of joint property goes to their beneficiaries, and all of the second partner's separate property and one half of joint property goes to his or her beneficiaries.

4. When one partner passes on, everything goes to the surviving partner, and when he or she passes on, everything is split in half with one half going to one partner's beneficiaries and the other half going to the other partner's beneficiaries

Let's use some examples to help make it clearer. Paul and Art are domestic partners, and they don't have any children. In putting together their joint revocable living trust, they decide they want to provide for each other. They have some different ideas to consider regarding who would receive their property after the second of them passes on. Paul has a sister Cecilia, and Art has a cousin Julio they each want to provide for.

In the first situation above, Paul and Art agree they want everything to go to each other first, and then sixty percent (60 percent) will go to Julio and forty percent (40 percent) will go to Cecilia. Regardless of how property is listed in the domestic partnership property agreement, they wish to do a 60-40 split among the two beneficiaries. This scenario is not that common except in situations where the partners have children, and in those cases, it is usually an equal division among the children.

In the second scenario above, Paul and Art wish to have everything go to the surviving partner should one of them pass on. After that, if Art was the surviving partner, then upon Art's passing, all of the property would go to Julio. If Paul was the surviving partner, then upon Paul's passing, all of the property would go to Cecilia. Because partners are usually planning together, they usually wish to jointly provide in some fashion for friends and family members together, so the "all or nothing" scenario is extremely rare.

In the third case above, Paul and Art have a domestic partnership property agreement with their trust and each has some separately accounted property and some joint property. (These domestic partnership property agreement provisions are already incorporated into The Estate Plan's Domestic Partner AB-SECURE™ Trust). Because Paul's career has been much more lucrative than Art's, Paul has more assets than Art. If Paul passes on first, then all of his separate property and his one-half of the joint property will be accessible to Art during his lifetime, but the assets will still be kept accounted for separately. When Art passes on, all of Paul's separately accounted property and his one-half of the joint property will go to Cecilia. All of Art's separately controlled property and the other half of the joint property will go to Julio.

In the forth instance above, Paul and Art are leaving everything to the surviving partner when one of them passes on. Regardless of who passes on first, the survivor will be able to use everything, and then upon his passing, everything would be split evenly between Cecilia and Julio.

These are merely four of the most popular distribution methods using only one alternate beneficiary for each partner. Life is not always this simple, and there are many more contingencies for which to plan. What would happen to Cecilia's inheritance if she passed on first? If it were to go to her children equally, what if one of them passed on? Would it go to her grandchildren? At what age?

A good partner protection planning attorney or advisor will press you for more and more contingencies until he or she gets into some fairly remote possibilities. If you are not throwing up your hands in frustration saying, "My God, if all of those people are dead then I just don't care anymore!" then they are not pressing you hard enough for these contingencies. Most of my clients get to the point where they don't have anyone else they wish to name, and then they are either fine with their "next of kin" getting their property, or they will leave it to a charity.

Here are some of the more "different" rules I have seen in my years as a life and estate planning attorney:

- An adult child in his 40s was not to receive everything all at once, but the mother did not want to say his inheritance would be tied up for the remainder of his life. Therefore, she compromised and said he could receive his entire inheritance free and clear when he turned one hundred and eighty-six years old (186.)

- No less than $50,000 was to be spent on a funeral and wake in Key West, including a liberal allowance for Jack Daniel's whiskey and other liquor.

- The first $1 million or 50% of the estate, whichever is less, is to be held in trust and used to establish a non-profit animal sanctuary for their pets in perpetuity.

- A tortoise named Lou Bob is to be donated to the Reptile House of San Diego Zoo (because it was likely the tortoise would outlive the couple and their teenaged children).

- A box of dirt is to be purchased and sent to the son-in-law as his sole inheritance.

As you can see, there is really no end to the kinds of bequests and conditions that can be created. It all depends on what the partners want.

Benefits of avoiding probate

There are a few extraordinarily important benefits of the revocable living trust directly related to avoiding probate. Because assets in a revocable living trust avoid probate, there are lower settlement costs, shorter settlement times and private distributions.

This is also a good place to talk about exactly why trust assets avoid probate. There are many attorneys and advisors who will tell you revocable living trusts avoid probate, but rarely will they tell you how it works. Well here's the big secret:

- Probate is nothing more than an elaborate process that re-titles assets.
- Probate takes assets that remain in the name of a person even after they have died and then distributes them to the proper beneficiaries.
- If nothing remains titled in the name of a deceased person, then there is no need for probate.
- When assets are titled in the name of the trust rather than an individual, when that person passes on, there is nothing to probate.

That's it. It's really that simple. Whenever assets are in a trust, they are technically in the name of the trust and not the deceased person. Because the trust assets are not in the name of the deceased person, there is no probate. Now that you know how assets in the revocable living trust avoid probate, we can briefly cover some the benefits of avoiding probate.

No probate means shorter settlement times. With the exception of shorter processes that some states allow for tiny estates, probate is a long, drawn out process. It is common for probate to take somewhere between nine months and two years to settle, and some estates drag on for considerably longer periods of time. For example, Elvis' probate started on December 20, 1977 when the will was admitted to the court, and it lasted through August 22, 1989 when the file was finally closed. In the end, the $10 million estate was reduced to about $3 million after fees and costs. While it is not likely your partner would have to wait 12 years for your assets to be available, there is no need to take any chances.

Avoiding probate also means avoiding extensive costs for appraisals, attorney fees and related costs of filling out unnecessary paperwork. While studies have varied on the exact costs, and it is different from state to state and jurisdiction to jurisdiction, the broad range costs may be between 4 percent and 10 percent of the estate assets. That can add up to some significant costs, which are not at all necessary.

Here are some estate values and corresponding estimated costs:

Estate Value	Estimated Costs
$100,000	$4,000-$10,000
$500,000	$20,000-$50,000
$1,000,000	$40,000-$100,000
$1,500,000	$60,000-$150,000
$2,000,000	$80,000-$200,000

At the time of this writing, some of the most comprehensive legal partner planning documents can be created for much less than $5,000, and chances are, if the costs are higher, it is because tax planning is involved. By the time both partners' estates are settled through the probate process, the costs above are doubled to account for two probates. Just in terms of cost savings, the trust is a better bet for all couples and even individuals, and considering all of the other benefits, it is a must for domestic partners.

Avoiding probate also means the settlement of your assets is private. In many states, probate court is like any other court where the filings are public documents. This means anyone can come off the street, see what assets you had when you died, who they are going to, and what that address is. Aside from the usual concerns of marketers, identity thieves and con artists seeing what accounts you had and the fact your partner is receiving them, many people feel it is simply no one's business. They're right.

I was once speaking with a financial advisor who provides workshops on revocable living trusts, and she always goes to the courthouse the morning before her workshop and gets copies of inventories for an estate that went through probate. At the workshop, she starts listing all of the personal information for the deceased person, the accounts and account balances on the date of death, and the names, addresses and dates of birth of all of the beneficiaries. During one of these workshops a man in the back row started screaming he knew the deceased woman and the presenter had no right to invade the privacy of her family like this. Well, that was exactly the point. She had every right to get the information because probate documents are public records. If you want to keep information private, then it should not go through probate.

By far, these three benefits in avoiding probate would be worth the cost and effort in establishing a revocable living trust. But there is even one more critical problem some domestic partners have that the revocable living trust can help solve.

Living trusts are more difficult to contest than wills

As mentioned earlier, it is statistically much more difficult to contest a revocable living trust than it is to contest a last will and testament. For many domestic partner couples, there is at least one family member they are at least a little concerned would create trouble. In some cases, there is outright hostility from at least one partner's family. Avoiding these conflicts usually tops the list for domestic partner planning priorities, so this is one more big benefit a revocable living trust has over a will.

Summary

The right revocable living trust can provide the means for domestic partners to bring their property together and manage it as one family unit, upon death distribute property to the people they chose, and provide age and other restrictions. Properly drafted, executed and funded revocable living trusts also can avoid all of the negatives of probate, including high costs, long settlement times, susceptibility to challenges and loss of privacy. By using the right revocable living trust as the base of their legal partner planning documents, domestic partners can achieve many of their goals. For more information on The Estate Plan's Domestic Partner AB-SECURE Trust, please download the free report at www.partnerabsecuretrust.com.

Chapter Four: The Domestic Partner Property Agreement

Jared and Justin sat across from the lawyer, admiring the paneled walls and gigantic oak desk. With a thick, gold-plated pen in his hand, he told them, "Of course, we should set up reciprocal Wills for the two of you," he said, nearly pointing at them with his pen. "That way you can inherit from each other."

With a quick glance at each other, Justin wrote something down on his note pad while Justin asked, "What about a joint revocable living trust?"

They knew the answer they were looking for. It was just not clear whether or not the attorney knew enough to provide them what they wanted. The attorney gave them a slightly annoyed/slightly questioning look. "Well, I supposed we could do that. Most of my clients with less than $2 million dollars do not need a revocable living trust, and they do just fine with Wills."

Justin continued to write on the notepad, and, without looking up, asked, "What about the house? It's currently paid up and is just in my name. How should it be titled?"

Tapping the expensive pen against the palm of his hand, the lawyer looked up as if searching for an answer. "Well, we can handle that one of two ways," the lawyer exhaled. "We could retitle the house as joint with a right of survivorship, or we could retitle it into the name of the joint trust you suggested. But I think it would be fine just to leave it alone and make provisions for it in the Wills."

Jared and Justin stopped and frowned at each other, trying not to be too obvious. "Well, we would prefer to avoid probate," Jared said, watching the lawyer frown a little. "Let's assume we go with the joint revocable living trust. What about the gift taxes in placing retitling the deed in the name of the trust?"

"What do you mean?" the lawyer asked.

"I mean," Jared said, "would you use a domestic partnership property agreement to avoid the gift tax problem?"

The lawyer looked at them more than a little confused, as if he had been asked whether or not the spaceship was picking him up at four o'clock or at five. Justin and Jared got up, thanked him for his time, and started walking out, noting the rows of books on probate procedures. Jared paused for a moment, sifted through some papers, and handed him his copy of Estate Planning for Domestic Partners. *"Here, you should probably read this before trying to help any more domestic partner couples," he said before they walked out the door to find another attorney.*

In the example above, Justin and Jared learned enough to ask the right questions. By the insistence in pursuing Wills and a strong leaning towards using the probate court system, it was pretty clear this lawyer was not for them. But even professionals who are skilled enough to see strong benefits in avoiding probate through a joint revocable living trust may not be knowledgeable enough to recognize problems with gift taxes on funding that joint trust. A critical part of having the *right* domestic partner revocable living trust is having a Domestic Partner Property Agreement that works with the trust. By having this agreement in place, domestic partners are able to combine their assets under one trust, but at the same time the agreement keeps the assets separate for tax purposes. (For an explanation of the gift tax, please download the free report at www.domesticpartnergifttaxes.com). The Domestic Partner AB-SECURE™ Trust through The Estate Plan™ integrates this essential agreement directly into the trust paperwork.

Combining assets without commingling them

Now that we've gone through the revocable living trust, choosing successor trustees and all of the reasons to have a joint trust for you and your partner, I can now reveal the big, secret method for combining property without violating the gift tax rules. After all, we have been recommending the assets of both partners be placed into the name of the living trust, but if these assets are not equal, it may trigger gift taxes. I'm about to tell you how it is done.

For those readers who are domestic partners looking into legal partner planning, this is a good thing for you to know when you speak with an attorney or advisor about a joint revocable living trust. For those life and estate planning attorneys who are typically recommending separate trusts because of the gift tax rules, here is the secret to successfully taking your practice up a notch and providing joint trusts for your domestic partner clients.

Most committed couples want to bring everything they have together so "what's yours is mine and what's mine is yours." However, directly mixing assets is a sure way to violate the gift tax rules we mentioned previously. A properly drafted joint revocable living trust in tandem with a domestic partnership property agreement can bring many of both partner's assets into the trust. Since both partners are trustees of the trust and both are beneficiaries of the trust, they can, with a few limitations, both utilize each other's assets.

As trustees, both partners are able to control everything in the trust. The assets will be listed in the domestic partnership property agreement depending on which partner contributed an asset. Both partners can take out money and spend it, buy and sell assets, make investment decisions for the other, and otherwise do anything their partner could do if it were still in his or her separate name with these exceptions and clarifications:

1) Whenever one partner takes an asset listed as the other partner's property in the domestic partnership property agreement, the partner is deemed to have used it in his or her capacity as a trustee.
2) It is OK to utilize the partner's assets for the good of the household, the partnership, or the partner individually.
3) It is not OK to take money from one partner's account and put it into the other partner's account without triggering the gift tax.

It is important for a domestic partnership property agreement to be incorporated into the overall plan to work with a joint revocable living trust for domestic partners and not just be an independent document. To leave no room for error, The Estate Plan™ incorporates this agreement directly into a Partner AB-SECURE™ Trust.

Example using agreement

Here's an example of how a domestic partnership property agreement works with the trust. Laverne and Shirley are partners who want to create a joint revocable living trust, and they want to put as many of their assets as they can into the trust so they can act as one family unit. They create the Laverne and Shirley Revocable Living Trust. They also have the following assets:

- condominium in Milwaukee owned by Laverne and Shirley jointly (and it was jointly purchased by them)
- townhouse in California owned by Shirley
- 40 percent ownership in the Pizza Bowl restaurant/bowling alley owned by Laverne
- $200,000 in Boo-Boo Kitty Mutual Fund owned by Shirley
- $100,000 in Big L Brokerage Fund owned by Laverne.

The condominium, townhouse, Pizza Bowl stock and both mutual funds will be transferred into the name of the trust. In the domestic partnership property agreement, the condominium in Milwaukee will be listed as joint trust assets. The townhouse in California and Boo-Boo Kitty Mutual Fund will be listed as Shirley's separately accounted property, and the Pizza Bowl stock and Big L Brokerage Fund will be listed as Laverne's separately accounted property.

Both Laverne and Shirley jointly control all of the property as trustees, but for tax purposes, the assets are accounted for as if they were still separate. In other words, Laverne will still pay dividend and capital gains taxes on her separate stock, Shirley will pay property taxes on her townhouse and dividend and capital gains taxes on her mutual fund, and both Laverne and Shirley will pay property taxes on their condominium in Milwaukee.

One note for joint property that is *not* owned 50 percent by each is that it is technically separate property. For example, if a stock fund is owned as sixty percent (60 percent) by Laverne and forty percent (40 percent) by Shirley, then the fund would be titled in the name of the trust. However, the domestic partnership property agreement would list the 60 percent ownership as the separate property of Laverne and 40 percent ownership as the separate property of Shirley. It *would not* list the account in the joint property section of the agreement.

Other provisions

In addition to keeping property accounted for separately within the joint revocable living trust, the domestic partnership property agreement also assists in the orderly dissolution of the trust if the partnership breaks up. In other words, it acts as a sort of "pre-nup" (pre-marital agreement) for domestic partners.

The standard dissolution terms are simple:

- Whatever the first partner has listed as separate property is hers to take.
- Whatever the second partner has listed as separate property is hers to take.
- All jointly owned property is divided equally between the partners.

The standard division of assets keeps separate property separate and divides joint property down the middle; this does not have to be the case. The agreement can be amended to provide a different form of asset division. However, it is important to keep in mind any unequal division may incur gift taxes if the "unequal" division exceeds $13,000 in the year of division.

While many domestic partner breakups can be handled amicably, this is not always the case. There are enough emotional difficulties associated with committed partners going separate ways, so having a guideline for dividing the property fairly and equitably can reduce the amount of stress (not to mention legal fees) in seeing the division made final.

Summary

While domestic partners typically want to combine assets as one family unit for legal partner planning purposes, a revocable living trust can offer an ideal solution. However, in order to avoid onerous gift and other tax complications, a domestic partner property agreement can account for property separately, avoid tax complications and also provide for a division of assets and dissolution of the trust in case the domestic partners break up. For more information on the federal gift tax please review the free report from the IRS at http://www.irs.gov/publications/p950/index.html.

Chapter Five: Ancillary Healthcare Documents

The woman sitting next to Gary was crying, and there didn't seem to be any end in sight. While he felt bad for her, he had problems of his own. His partner Mitch had collapsed yesterday, and an ambulance had rushed him to the hospital. It had already been 24 hours, and Mitch had come in and out of consciousness.

At first, the doctors had refused to give Gary any answers because he was not family. They had already called Mitch's family to come in when Gary had given them a copy of the healthcare power of attorney. Now it was the family that was not getting any answers unless they got them from Gary. In particular, Mitch's father had always rejected Gary and flatly refused to even consider that Mitch was "that way." And he did cause a huge scene in the waiting room when the doctor refused to follow his instructions instead of Gary. Now, Mitch's father only gave him the occasional dirty look across the waiting room. It was amazing what a small piece of paper could do to remedy a colossally bad situation.

The doctor came in to the waiting room and walked right to Gary, ignoring the questions of Mitch's father and brother. "Good news," he said to Gary. "Mitch is now fine and asking to talk with you. You can see him in a few minutes."

Gary sat back with a wave of relief. He had almost forgotten the woman was sitting next to him when she said "I'm glad to hear its good news… I have no idea what's going on with my partner."

She seemed to be coming out of the cry a little, and she continued "We've been together for ten years, but they didn't care how long we were together," she said calmly. "We even had a commitment ceremony. Debbie's sister hates her, but that's who they're asking for medical instructions."

She directly at Gary and he tried to give a sympathetic grin back, but it was tough. "Don't they understand that Debbie would want me to make decisions for her?"

Gary looked back at her and gently asked, "Didn't you show them Debbie's healthcare power of attorney?"

The shocked look on her face was all the answer Gary needed. Apparently, they had never got around to making one.

In addition to The Domestic Partner AB-SECURE Trust™ and the Domestic Partnership Property Agreement, there are a several documents critical t to domestic partners putting together a comprehensive legal partner plan. They are:

- A Healthcare Power of Attorney
- A Living Will
- A Financial Power of Attorney
- Nomination of Conservator

Without at least these documents to augment a living trust and property agreement, domestic partners are definitely skating on thin ice. We'll examine the Healthcare Power of Attorney and Living Will in this section and the Financial Power of Attorney and Nomination of Conservator in the next chapter.

Healthcare Power of Attorney and Living Will

One of the most common horror stories for domestic partners revolves around one partner falling ill and the other not being allowed to make medical decisions, or worse, not even being allowed to visit the partner in the hospital. The number of stories is vast, and it is profoundly disturbing that a partner of 40 years is suddenly swept aside in favor of long-estranged relatives to make medical decisions.

There has been a lot of bad advice out there in certain aspects of legal partner planning, but thankfully one of those areas has not been about healthcare powers of attorney and living wills. Perhaps due to the horror stories as well as to the lack of legal rights and societal acceptance, gay and lesbian couples have been ahead of unmarried couples in embracing these documents. The healthcare power of attorney allows a person to appoint agents to make healthcare decisions when he or she is not able to do so. These decisions can encompass everything from the simple choice of whether either brand-name or generic aspirin should be given to the patient, up to the gut-wrenching decision of whether or not life support should be withdrawn.

A living will (sometimes referred to as an advance healthcare directive), contains specific orders from the patient, written in advance, regarding course of treatment if the person is in a persistent vegetative state, is terminal and incurable or is considered by the state to be incapable of giving informed consent. Some states use a living will less as your own orders and more as a specific appointment of someone to make just life support decisions for you.

A complete set of directives should include a healthcare power of attorney and living will. These directives should address the following areas:

- A successive list of the people; i.e., your agents, to make healthcare decisions for you

- When the power of attorney agent is allowed to make decisions for you

- How the power of attorney is rescinded
- The general and specific statements of the authority granted
- A statement regarding any powers which are specifically *not* granted to the power of attorney
- Clauses limiting liability for medical professionals as well as third parties if they rely on the power of attorney
- Directions on how to proceed if you are on life support and artificial nutrition and there is no hope of recovery.

Before going into the specifics of a healthcare power of attorney, it is important to note different states have different rules, and your state's rules may be different. Something that is universal among all 50 states is if you do not have a healthcare power of attorney, then the state provides you with one, and it is usually your "next of kin." These various state statutes are what give relatives precedence over a domestic partner in making medical decisions because, once again, you are not legally married. (Thankfully at the time of this writing, this is not the case in Massachusetts, Connecticut, Vermont and Iowa, since gay and lesbian couples are allowed to marry, but family members are the next "next of kin" after your partner and if you are traveling outside of those states, it is likely your marriage right to make medical decisions will not be honored.) Whether you reside in these states or not, you may have other people you wish to name as alternate agents instead of abiding by your state's definition of next of kin. That is why everyone, even married couples, should have these documents.

Choosing your healthcare agents

The primary decision when putting together a healthcare power of attorney is choosing who will be your agents. The best piece of advice I can give is to name only one person at a time. A central reason for a healthcare power of attorney is to make it absolutely clear who is making decisions if you cannot do it yourself. Naming two or three people to act together is a recipe for discord and confusion. Imagine a doctor having a healthcare power of attorney with three agents listed as acting together. The doctor gets an order from one agent, a second agent shows up and gives a contradictory order, and then the third shows up and wants the doctor to do something completely different. Having one agent acting at a time solves this problem by having one clear voice to speak on your behalf at this critical time.

I know what some of you are thinking. "Well, after my partner, I have three children (or nieces or nephews, or brothers and sisters, etc.) and I don't want any of them to feel left out. I love them all equally."

As an attorney who has been counseling clients for more than a decade on powers of attorney, I understand the arguments. But what we are talking about is your health and your life—not whether or not one person got a better Christmas present, or whether or not you gave one of them more money over the years, and certainly not whom you love best. At this most critical of times, you need to select the best person for the job first, the second best person for the job second, and so on. It has nothing to do with loving people unequally, and it has everything to do with choosing the person who will be the best healthcare agent for you.

So who would be the best healthcare agent? Domestic partners usually know their partner is first on their list, but where they run into trouble is selecting the successor agents. I usually give my clients a little direction on choosing their agents. Choose someone who:

- generally thinks the way you do about medical decisions and healthcare

- is medically knowledgeable, or at least is medically curious and will look into your situation

- has no trouble seeking a second opinion or firing a doctor.

Considering someone who generally thinks the way you do on medical decisions and healthcare can give a little or a lot of weight in choosing or denying certain people as your agent. For some people, this may mean choosing trusted people in your particular religion so they can make medical decisions in line with your religious practices. In other cases, it may mean you wish to rely on prescription medication as little as possible and therefore you want someone knowledgeable about alternative medicines. The main point is to pick someone who generally thinks as you do regarding medicine.

The second factor is making sure your agents are medically knowledgeable, or at least medically curious. The second part of that sentence is probably more important than the first. The person you want making medical decisions for you should take the time to look into the medical treatments recommended, do some research, and then ask intelligent questions of the doctor, possibly even challenging the physician. Recent studies suggest there are an appalling number of times a doctor or nurse administers the wrong medication or the wrong dose, sometimes resulting in medical tragedies or death. It is important you have a healthcare agent who will be an informed second set of eyes making sure everything runs smoothly as you recover.

Finally, your healthcare agent should be bold enough to stand up to a doctor, get a second opinion if he or she thinks it is warranted, and be able to fire a doctor if necessary. It does you no good to choose a person who thinks as you do, will look into medical matters to make sure everything is going well, but if he realizes something is wrong, he is too timid to bring it up with the doctor. You don't need someone who is belligerent, but at the same time, the person should not be afraid to get a second opinion.

When Power of Attorney agents should act

In order for a healthcare agent to start making decisions for you, you have to be no longer able to make decisions for yourself. So, breathe a little easier. By creating a power of attorney for healthcare decisions, you are not giving up your right to make those decisions yourself. It is only if you are not able to make decisions or communicate them that you let someone else make the decisions for you.

But when are you considered to be "not able" or "incapacitated" for these purposes? The power of attorney would outline the conditions, or if not, then state law would decide when you are incapacitated. In general, it is preferable for you to determine in the healthcare power of attorney exactly what triggers the power of attorney to act. The alternative may be a court proceeding in which a judge has to weigh evidence and testimony, and that may be a costly, complicated procedure. Most healthcare powers of attorney, even the office supply store versions, will list the conditions under which the power of attorney is active. It may be as simple as stating if "any attending physician" certifies in writing you are not able to make your own healthcare wishes known, then the power of attorney becomes active and your agent can act on your behalf.

There are also some choices available to you in the power of attorney document. You may also specifically designate one or more physicians to make the determination. If you have had the same doctor for 20 years and feel comfortable with him or her, then you may want that physician to specifically make that determination. But this choice also comes with a word of caution. It may be a longer procedure than you think, and it may be expensive to have your regular physician make the diagnosis if you are on the other side of the country when the diagnosis is needed. You should always weigh the comfort you have with a particular physician against the flexibility which may be needed in given situations. If my clients are given any guidance, almost all decide to keep things flexible and simply state any two attending physicians may make this certification in writing.

How a Power of Attorney is rescinded

Just as important as when a healthcare power of attorney is active is when and how it is revoked. Just as "when" an agent may act is written in the document, the method of revoking the power of attorney should also be written into it.

While the process may be as elaborate as having to execute a new power of attorney, it is recommended you keep it simpler than that. The process also should not be so simple that there are no formalities at all, such as saying "I revoke my healthcare power of attorney." Having things this simple opens the door to meddling family members lying and declaring you verbally rescinded your power of attorney in a "moment of clarity." Now all of the court proceedings you hoped to avoid can spring up. The simplest balance is to have the revocation of a healthcare power of attorney in writing.

Authorities granted to your agent

Now that you have appointed healthcare agents and decided when the power of attorney is active and rescinded, it is time to determine exactly what authority your agent will have. In general, it is recommended his or her powers be extensive so the individual can handle any situation that arises. Each healthcare power of attorney should list at least the following powers:

- Information — the ability to receive and review medical records; the ability to consent to the disclosure of medical records; and the ability to sign all consent and other forms necessary to carry out the other powers

- Manage Health Professionals — the ability to hire and fire medical professionals; the ability to admit and discharge you from medical facilities; and the ability to consent or withhold consent for all medications and procedures

- Releases — Clauses limiting liability for medical professionals, as well as third parties if they rely on the power of attorney
- Life Support — the ability to authorize or withhold life support and other treatment if you are in certain terminal and incurable conditions.

Information

One of the most important clauses of a healthcare power of attorney is the ability to receive and review medical records. After all, it does you and your partner no good to have all of the other powers if the partner has nothing on which to base his or her decision. It is also critical your partner be allowed to release the medical records to other medical practitioners so her or she can make their best recommendations and care for you.

Imagine a doctor asking you to approve an operation for you partner, but the doctor cannot disclose any medical information to you, explain why it is necessary, or what the possible risks and side effects would be. I can't imagine approving the repair of my car without all of the facts, let alone making a decision about someone's health.

Part of granting this authority should also specifically include a waiver of privacy rights under the Health Insurance Portability and Accountability Act of 1996. The law, while good for patient privacy on many levels, also put roadblocks in place that made most healthcare powers of attorney ineffective by denying healthcare agents access to necessary medical information. My firm includes HIPAA waiver language in all of our powers of attorney, but The Estate Plan™ and some other attorneys prefer to execute waivers as a separate form. Either method works to give your agent the authority he or she needs to take care of your health.

It is also important to include the power to sign all consent forms on your behalf, and this is probably the power that will be utilized most often. In an age where medicine is governed by bureaucracy, there are many forms to sign, so it is standard practice to give your healthcare agent the broadest possible authority to sign consent forms.

Manage health professionals

The ability to receive or refuse medical treatment and the ability to engage and discharge medical professionals are hallmarks of our healthcare system. If you believe your doctor is not acting competently or if you just don't like the doctor, you always have the ability to fire him or her. If you want to try an experimental treatment or if you object to receiving blood transfusions, you have the right to consent to or refuse specific medical treatments and medications. And if you are unable to exercise these rights, it is critical that your agent exercise them for you.

Part of being able to manage health professionals also includes the power to admit and discharge you from hospitals, nursing facilities and other places of medical treatment. If you admit yourself to a hospital and, because of the negligence of the hospital you become incapacitated, you would want your partner to be able to get you out of that hospital and into a new one as quickly as possible.

Releases

Some important terms for making sure orders given by your partner and other healthcare agents are obeyed are clauses releasing medical professionals, hospitals and others from any and all liability for obeying your agent. The main concern here is doctors and hospitals do not want to be sued for following your healthcare agent's order.

Imagine a situation where you were involved in a car accident and are unconscious. The emergency room doctors examine you and determine you need one of two operations to save your life. One, if successful, is 100 percent likely to save your life but it involves amputating your leg. The other, which the doctors recommend, is 80 percent likely to save your life and does not involve any amputations. Your healthcare agent wants to authorize the first operation with the amputation.

At this point, the doctors, hospital and others involved in providing medical care are worried once you regain consciousness you will sue them for the amputation of your leg. In order to make it easy for them to accept the orders of your chosen agent without question or seeking a court order to follow their directions, they want to confirm they will not be held liable for obeying your agent's orders. For this reason, extensive language is usually incorporated into healthcare powers of attorney releasing just about everyone from liability for obeying your agent. This language does not release anyone from liability for being negligent or for medical malpractice, only from being liable for following instructions of the healthcare agent.

Life support

Another component of a healthcare power of attorney is a general statement about life support and artificial nutrition. Many people do not want to be "hooked up to machines" or "fed through a tube" if there is no hope of recovery. Others want to hang on for as long as technology will s their body functioning. It does not matter which choice you make as long as you also list these wishes in writing in the power of attorney.

Writing out these wishes will give your agents and physicians clear direction on what you want to have done. It is then up to your agent to authorize your wishes and the medical professionals to carry out the wishes. The other way to handle this difficult decision is to make it ahead of time in a living will.

Living Will

The living will may be the simplest document in a legal partner plan, but it may turn out to be the most important one for your partner and loved ones to have. Although the healthcare power of attorney allows your partner and others to make medical decisions for you, the living will takes the final, most difficult decision out of their hands. When it comes to whether or not to administer life support and artificial nutrition and hydration at the end of life, a living will can express your wishes and directions.

There are two very powerful reasons to have a living will. First, it expresses your wishes should you ever get to the point where doctors would ask if they should "pull the plug." Actually, doctors have much more tactful ways of expressing things in these situations, but we can get right to the point. What you want in this situation is not clear unless you have it in writing, and a living will does that for you.

Keep in mind that marriage does not necessarily solve this problem either. Remember the Terry Schiavo case? She was married, but her husband and parents battled for 15 years over what she wanted. Had her wishes been in writing, her family would not have had all those battles where the family only got grief and the only people who benefited were the lawyers.

The second reason for having a living will is for the benefit of your partner, friends and family members. By placing your orders to a doctor in writing and in the proper format under state law, you take the burden of making that decision from your loved ones. In legal terms, the living will overrides your healthcare power of attorney because it is a specific document with a specific order for a specific situation, and, depending on the state, can be taken right from the statutes.

It is important to note most states allow a living will to make the determination ahead of time, so as long as your attending physicians (or even a specific doctor chosen by you) determines there is no hope of recovery and your body is only being kept going by machines, then your wishes will be followed. Other states do not allow this kind of order to be made and instead insist a person chosen by you make the decision for you at the time. Until those states catch up with the others, you can still make your wishes known in a living will, but your chosen agent will have to make the decision for you.

How the Living Will works with the Healthcare Power of Attorney

By using a healthcare power of attorney, you have most likely stated your wishes are covered by a living will. Either you want life support and artificial nutrition or not. But this is merely language to give your agent direction should you ever fall that ill. The living will is an *order* from you on what needs to be done, signed under the formalities imposed by state law, and should be presented to the doctors directly.

In short, the healthcare power of attorney covers all healthcare decisions you would be able to make yourself except for the last, most difficult one. That decision is expressed in your living will. *Not even your healthcare power of attorney agent can override your decision.*

It is with this last part that some couples, whether married or not, express some reservations. There is quite naturally conflict between the desire to take this incredible burden off your partner and make the decision ahead of time, and yet there is a desire to not let your partner feel helpless to stop doctors from removing medical treatment that is keeping your body functioning. In these situations, the decision comes down to whether or not to have a living will at all. If there is no living will, then your designated agent makes the decision for you.

Will doctors honor these documents?

I would like to say doctors and hospitals will follow the law, but it is not always the case. The law *requires* doctors to follow the directives in a healthcare power of attorney and living will, but sometimes doctors ignore the law and turn to the next of kin, out of habit, convenience or prejudice. In these cases, it is important for your partner or other agent to make it very clear he or she will institute legal action to have your documents enforced. (Again, this is another reason to choose a healthcare agent who will stand up to a doctor). A court can review the documents and issue an order forcing the doctor to accept the orders of your directives.

Summary

While domestic partners face many inequities under the law, making healthcare decisions for each other does not have to remain one of them. Having a properly created and executed healthcare power of attorney and living will can help partners seize the power to protect each other should a partner fall ill. For more information on healthcare powers of attorney and other medical documents, please visit the domestic partner section of www.livingtrustlawfirm.com. For specific information on healthcare directives in your state, contact an attorney knowledgeable in life and estate planning.

Chapter Six: Ancillary Financial Documents

"I'm sorry, I can't do anything for you," the snarky teller told Samantha, handing back the piece of paper. "Your name is not on this account, and I can't do anything about it."

"That's not what I was told," Samantha sniped back. And with good reason. Her partner Catherine had fallen victim to a stroke, and while an almost full recovery was expected, it would be months before she would be able to handle banking or other business dealings.

They had put together a Domestic Partner AB-SECURE Trust with a Domestic Partnership Property Agreement, and they had transferred most of their accounts into the trust. What they had not gotten around to yet was transferring their checking and savings accounts into the trust, and while Samantha could liquidate some stock to handle the bills, she would really rather not.

Samantha had nearly drained her own checking and savings accounts handling the bills, and when she talked with her attorney, she advised Samantha to use the Financial Power of Attorney to access Catherine's accounts. "That's what it is for," their attorney said.

Now the bank teller was refusing to help. "Get your manager," Samantha told, rather than asked, the teller, giving her the power of attorney back.

She was still fuming when she started to hear the manager and the teller arguing, but she couldn't quite make out everything.

"… says she's some kind of partner, *or whatever they call it these days…"*

"…looks like it's in order…"

"…not family and she's not on the account…"

"It's an original, signed and notarized power of attorney," the manager said a lot more loudly. "We will *honor it, and we could get in a lot of trouble if we didn't."*

Trying not to look like she overheard, Samantha waited patiently as the manager came to the front counter to help. "I'm sorry about that," he said as he approached her. "The power of attorney looks valid, and we will follow your instructions. Let's go to my office and have you fill out a few forms and then we can give you access to your partner's accounts."

Samantha went with the manager, not being able to control throwing a sly grin to the teller as she walked away.

While there are many horror stories about partners not being able to make healthcare decisions for each other, there are just as many that involve a partner falling ill, the estranged family stepping in and before you know it, the other partner is out on the street. This is a particularly difficult situation if the partner who falls ill is the provider and the other is the homemaker. Unless legal steps are taken, the family members, as heartless as they may be, could be within their legal rights to do just that.

The ideal solution comes in the form of a Domestic Partner AB-SECURE Trust, but the financial control under the trust is only for assets and accounts owned *within* the trust. Retirement accounts are specifically held outside of the trust, and other assets and benefits are controlled by employers and government entities. In order for a partner to take control of these assets in an emergency, legally proper financial documents like a financial power of attorney and nomination of conservator are needed to handle those situations that are not covered by the trust.

Financial Power of Attorney

The easiest solution for partners is to name each other as agents in their financial power of attorney documents. As power of attorney, the partner can manage the assets of the sick partner and still have access to their home and finances without worrying the "next of kin" will be able to go to court and take over. But just in case they do take matters to court, it is also recommended partners execute a nomination of a conservator or similar document so if a judge feels compelled to give someone legal "guardianship" over your partner, then your partner has a list of people he or she would choose.

Financial documents should have a financial power of attorney and a nomination of a conservator, and between them they should address the following areas:

- a successive list of the people to make financial decisions for you
- when the power of attorney agent can act
- general and specific statements of the authority granted
- statement regarding any powers specifically *not* granted to the power of attorney
- clauses limiting liability for financial institutions as well as third parties if they rely on the power of attorney
- nominations of conservators if a proceeding is instituted to assign one.

This list should look vaguely familiar when compared to the chapter on healthcare directives. This is because the same elements need to go into both healthcare and financial powers of attorney even though they are covering two very different areas.

Financial Power of Attorney (FPOA)

There are many names for a financial power of attorney. A nondurable power of attorney, a durable power of attorney or a springing power of attorney are some terms you may have heard. These and other specially named powers of attorney refer to the same exact powers; the names refer to when they are active.

A nondurable power of attorney is active while the principal, meaning the person whose power of attorney it is, is competent. It becomes inactive if the principal is deemed incompetent. (In all of my years of handling life and estate planning matters, I have never had a client who wanted this type of power of attorney, since people generally want someone to act for them if they can't. But it is out there.) A durable power of attorney, sometimes called a general power of attorney, refers to a power of attorney that is active while the principal is competent and then also remains active after a person becomes incompetent. A springing power of attorney only becomes active after the principal becomes incapacitated.

To keep things simple and understandable, we will avoid using these terms and instead generally call these documents financial powers of attorney. As for when they are active, we will also specifically discuss this since many clients want a blend of the durable and springing power of attorney, depending on which agent is named.

Choosing your financial agents

The most important part of drafting a financial power of attorney is deciding who will make decisions for you. As with the healthcare power of attorney, I also recommend only naming one person at a time to avoid conflicting decisions or needing more than one person to sign documents to get things done for you. While you may want your partner and your brother to work together to make financial decisions, it may be next to impossible to have them go to the bank together each and every time something needs to be signed.

Who would make good financial power of attorney agents? Partners usually name each other first, and then I generally advise my clients to agree on an agent who:

- is a person they trust with their assets and their life
- is financially knowledgeable but not necessarily an accountant or financial advisor
- knows when it is time to get financial help and can work with professionals.

The first criterion is the most important, because if you cannot trust the person with your money and your livelihood, then there is no need to look into the other two factors. While there are many financially qualified people who can do a good job at managing your finances if you fall ill, you first have to trust the person.

Second is to select someone who is financially knowledgeable but not necessarily an accountant or financial advisor. If the person can balance a checkbook and make practical decisions in spending money, then that is good enough. You are not asking your financial power of attorney agent to do your taxes or create an investment portfolio. You are only asking him or her to handle your bills, preserve your assets, and work with the right professionals to get those items done.

Finally, you should jointly choose a financial power of attorney agent who knows when it is time to hire a professional to help. There are people who are "chronic do-it-yourselfers." They may insist on handling all aspects of your finances, even those things you usually passed off to your CPA or financial advisor, out of stubbornness or a belief that by doing it themselves they are saving you money. Unfortunately, they could end up placing your finances in jeopardy. The agent you want is someone who can handle the everyday spending decisions and manage the professionals to keep your finances moving and growing while you are ill.

When a Power of Attorney agent should act

As mentioned before, there are three main time frames for when a power of attorney agent can act—both while you are competent and incompetent, only after you become incompetent and not before, or only while you are competent and not if you become incompetent. In determining when your agents should act, you should keep these situations in mind.

For most domestic partners, when they name each other as the first agent, there is value in having a durable power of attorney, which is active both now and if one becomes incapacitated. This allows domestic partners to act for each other the same married couples do. If the cable bill is in Will's name and the telephone account is under Vince's, each can make changes because they are the power of attorney. For more time sensitive matters, if Vince has to suddenly go out of town and they are scheduled to refinance their home, Will can simply use the power of attorney and sign for both. If one becomes incapacitated, then the other partner can continue to handle the couple's financial transactions.

While it is convenient for domestic partners to name each other as their first agents and have the power of attorney active all of the time, this is not necessarily what the partners want for successor agents. It is more common for people to want a successor agent to act only if they are unable to handle things themselves.

What does incapacitated mean?

Determining if the power of attorney is active can depend on whether or not someone is incapacitated. Exactly what does "incapacitated" mean? State laws vary on what this means, and states have different procedures to determine whether or not someone is incapacitated. But most of those procedures involve some court action, and that is precisely what we want to avoid. Instead, we can define "incapacitated" in the document itself.

In all cases, you want to make sure the definition of incapacitated is simple enough that it does not require a court to declare you incompetent, but at the same time it should be based upon solid medical evidence. The Estate Plan™ uses the following language in some of their power of attorney documents to define incapacity: "Principal shall be deemed incapacitated if at any time two (2) licensed physicians certify in writing that Principal has become physically or mentally disabled and is unable to manage his affairs in his best interest, whether or not a court of competent jurisdiction has declared Principal disabled, mentally ill or in need of a conservator/guardian."

The language does not have exact medical parameters, but it is clear any time two physicians state you can't take care of things yourself and put their determination in writing, you are incapacitated and unable to handle things yourself. It is also just as easy to determine you are competent to handle things again when two physicians certify in writing you are once again competent.

Authorities granted to your agent

We've looked at choosing financial agents and how and when the powers of attorney are active. Now we should look at the powers granted to the agent and what they can do on your behalf. In general, it is recommended financial powers be extensive so your agent can address issues as they arise. At a minimum, the document should list the following powers:

- general powers granted by statute
- handle tax matters
- make gifts
- change beneficiaries or re-title accounts or other assets
- purchase insurance or other financial products

General powers granted by statute

State laws usually spell out a list of powers a power of attorney agent or conservator can exercise, but most state laws do not cover everything needed. Nonetheless, it is a good idea to reference these powers as being part of the power of attorney. From this base, you can always add more powers.

Handle tax matters

An important part of being a power of attorney agent is handling all of your tax matters, including a few items that might not be incorporated into a general statement of authority or your state's statutes. In addition to simply being able to fill out and file tax returns, your agent should be able to get copies of past returns, settle any debts with the IRS or the state's department of revenue, file extensions, and claim refunds. In short, everything you can do as a taxpayer to interact with various government authorities should be included as part of the power of attorney.

Make gifts

While this may seem like something you would not want your power of attorney agent to do, it is actually critical he or she be allowed to if you were ever severely disabled and needed nursing home or similar care. As domestic partners, you are not able to claim certain exemptions as married couples would, and if you needed long-term care, you would have to exhaust your assets before Medicaid and other programs would take over the payments. (This is also a reason why we recommend our clients look into long-term care insurance).

While the rules are pretty strict regarding gifts, if there is time to transfer your assets to your partner using the power of attorney, you may be able to save some of those assets from having to be sold to pay for the long-term care facility. As a word of caution, do not try to handle applying for Medicaid or other programs without the assistance of an attorney or other professional who knows the rules. It can be extremely easy to make a costly mistake, so paying an attorney to help is well worth the price to save some of your assets.

Domestic partners may also wish to have this power to equalize their assets, even if one partner is incapacitated, to avoid future estate taxes. This topic is covered more fully in Chapter Fourteen, but for now it simply adds to the reasons in having your power of attorney incorporate gifting powers.

Change beneficiaries and re-title accounts

This power is particularly important if you and your partner have a revocable living trust and you need to change beneficiaries or title to property to fully fund your trust. In order to avoid probate, it is important your trust own your assets or list your trust as a "pay on death" or similar beneficiary.

If assets are in your individual name and need to be in the trust, then your agent needs the ability to re-title the asset by changing the account ownership or executing a new deed. If an asset like life insurance is still listing a person (even your partner) as your beneficiary, then the beneficiary would need to be changed to your revocable living trust.

Purchase insurance or other financial products

Just as with gifting, it may be in your and your partner's best interests to have this power in your document in case you need long-term or nursing home care. To make things simple and to preserve your assets, your agent could liquidate some of your assets and purchase an insurance annuity. An annuity is simply a type of life insurance with an investment portfolio attached to it which can be "annuitized."

When an annuity is annuitized, the insurance is cancelled with the company keeping all of the investments but in exchange they agree to pay you a set amount each month for the remainder of your life, no matter how long that may be. Your power of attorney agent can work with the insurance company to buy an annuity that will provide a monthly payment which covers all of your long-term care costs, and then the rest of your assets can be reserved for your partner.

While some of these situations may seem far-fetched right now, there is little reason to take these powers out of the documents just because you think it might not happen to you or your partner. When explaining some of these powers and other protective language to our clients, we usually call them "spare tire" clauses. Just because you don't expect to get a flat tire on the way to the grocery store does not mean you take the spare tire out of the car. It's there if you need it, and if you don't need it, then it's simply words on paper.

Statement regarding any powers specifically not granted to the power of attorney

While in most cases there are very few powers you should deny your agent, the option is there for you. In practice, it is best to give your power of attorney agent as much authority as possible. It is also a good idea to have a section to list those powers even if your answer is "NONE," meaning there are no powers you are denying to your agent.

If you are choosing to exclude any powers from the document, be sure you understand precisely the powers you wish to exclude, the reasons for excluding the power, and the consequences of if you end up in a situation where that power is needed. Be sure to talk this through with your attorney when putting the document together since, if he or she is a good attorney, he or she would be able to give you some examples of why the power is needed.

Releases

Just as it is important to release medical professionals from liability for obeying the orders of your healthcare agent, it is just as important to release financial institutions from liability for listening to your power of attorney agent. Again, the financial or other institution wants to make sure you will not regain the ability to act for yourself and then sue them for taking the orders of your agent if something does not go exactly as planned.

If your stockbroker took an order from your agent to sell one stock and purchase another and the second stock tanked, the stockbroker would not want you to come back and sue them for making the transaction. Therefore, unless the stockbroker is assured her or she will not be held liable for the bad decisions of your agent, the stockbroker would never accept the power of attorney in the first place. To make sure your agent will be listened to and obeyed, it is essential to have this release language in the document.

Do not misunderstand the meaning of the release language. If your stockbroker did something negligent or reckless, or even stole from you, this language would not protect him or her. All this language does is prevent you from suing them because they took orders from your assigned power of attorney agent. It is nothing more than that.

Summary

Healthcare Powers of Attorney and Financial Powers of Attorney are critical components of a legal domestic partner plan. Through them, you and your partner can establish even more power for each other than married couples get by signing a marriage certificate. It is critical to make sure your powers of attorney are complete, so be sure to review these points with your attorney. For added protection, be sure you and your partner have nomination of conservator documents just in case a judge feels compelled to poke their way into your affairs. For more information on healthcare documents used in partner planning, please go to www.livingtrustlawfirm.com and go to the domestic partners section. Again, for specific advice on your situation and with questions on the law, please contact an attorney in your state or jurisdiction.

Chapter Seven:
A Complete Partner Protection Plan

"And this is what we call The Big Blue Binder," I said, laying the massive book on the table. "In here, we have all of the legal documents you need to achieve the goals we discussed, both during life and after you have gone."

As I opened up the binder, I watched as Kathryn and Sherry leaned in, interested in the contents. Like so many others, the middle-aged couple had been together for years and thought they were covered with a set of simple wills. Then they read my book Estate Planning for Domestic Partners, attended a seminar I presented for a community group, and were only now seeing that they could have so much more even without gay marriage.

"That's an awful lot of paper," Kathryn said, looking impressed and questioning at the same time. "Is this really going to cover everything?"

I started going through the different sections of the binder one by one, pointing out the purpose of each document as well as the extras included with the trust. In addition to all of the essential legal documents, there were sections for recording final wishes regarding funeral arrangements, organizing financial summaries, recording trust allocations, and archiving deeds, account summaries and life insurance policies.

"The binder can be a place simply for storing your legal documents, or it can become an integral part of your life and financial planning," I explained. "Some of my clients use this book as the centerpiece in all of their dealings with their financial advisor, accountant, and attorney. They keep their financial account information here, copies of their most recent tax returns, their life insurance policies and property deeds. One couple even keeps a journal of their progress on New Year's resolutions each year."

As Kathryn and Sherry started flipping through the sample binder, they came across a section with fill-in-the-blanks regarding final instructions regarding memorial services. Suddenly, Sherry started to tear up. As an attorney working with clients on planning for the best and worst, I have come across many emotional clients. But this was the first time I had someone tear up at the sight of a checklist.

Kathryn, obviously understanding something I didn't, started hugging Sherry while looking towards me to explain. "Sherry was very close with her mother, and last year when she passed on Sherry was put in charge of all of the services," Kathryn said. "She arranged for a burial, church service, the music, everything."

"And it wasn't what she wanted at all," Sherry said, pulling out a tissue and wiping her eyes. "About three weeks after the service, we found a letter in her dresser giving specific instructions on everything she wanted to have done. Cremation, simple wake, specific songs for the funeral, everything."

Kathryn went on to explain that Sherry's mother and father had all of the "recommended" basic legal planning documents, "But there were a lot of holes to fill in, account statements to find, and other details Sherry had to figure out," she said.

Sherry finally recovered fully. "At least our children won't have to guess at our wishes," she said smiling, and began tapping the blue binder. "It will all be laid out right here."

Sherry's case is not that different from a lot of children's in dealing with their parents passing on, with the exception that Sherry actually found a list of instructions long after it was too late to do anything about it. But having a complete plan, with details filled in and all in one place, is extremely important.

Putting the details down in one place for your partner and loved ones to find can make dealing with the details of your passing a lot easier to handle… and give them more time to reflect on the good times with you.

Here are the documents needed for a complete legal domestic partner plan:

- The Domestic Partner AB-SECURE Trust with accompanying Domestic Partnership Property Agreement
- Financial and Healthcare Powers of Attorney
- Living Will/Advance Directives
- Nomination of Conservator Documents
- Pour-Over Wills
- Nomination of Guardianship Forms
- Assignment of Personal Effects Form

The Domestic Partner AB-SECURE Trust with accompanying Domestic Partnership Property Agreement

As the core of any effective legal domestic partner plan, the Domestic Partner AB-SECURE Trust controls most assets, and it provides financial and legal empowerment to both partners over all of their combined assets. If a partner falls ill, the well partner handles all financial matters dealing with assets in the trust. If a partner passes on, the access to trust assets is immediate, and full inheritance is nearly immediate. Further, when the second partner passes on, all of the contingent inheritance plans for both partners are spelled out in detail.

To summarize the general benefits of revocable living trust planning compared to Wills as outlined in Chapter Three, by avoiding probate administrative costs of between four and ten percent are saved, time delays of months or years are avoided, estate contests are stonewalled, and privacy is retained. And having the Domestic Partnership Property Agreement in place and properly utilized can allow both partners to combine their assets as one family unit while avoiding the onerous gift tax. The specially designed Domestic Partner AB-SECURE Trust available through The Estate Plan provides all of these benefits and more, including the remaining documents listed in this chapter. (www.theestateplan.com).

Financial and Healthcare Powers of Attorney

While the Domestic Partner AB-SECURE Trust allows one partner to handle most financial assets belonging to their sick partner, the Healthcare Power of Attorney allows the partner to make all medical decisions during their partner's incapacity. Some of the most important decisions an ailing person wants their partner to make relate to medical rather than financial or legal, including decisions regarding medication, hiring and firing of doctors, and visitation during hospital stays. The Healthcare Power of Attorney, while far simpler than the revocable living trust or Financial Power of Attorney, may become the most important document during a crisis.

Regarding financial and legal matters, the Domestic Partner AB-SECURE Trust is designed to handle all assets within the trust, but sometimes there are accounts and property held outside of the trust either by accident or by design. The type of account most often left outside of the trust is the retirement account. As explained in the Chapter on Managing The Trust, retirement accounts can not be retitled into the name and control of the trust without losing their tax-deferred status. In other words, if a retirement account is retitled in the name of a revocable living trust, then it is treated as if the entire account where withdrawn in one year with all of the income taxes and penalties due.

This is where a financial power of attorney can come in handy. By leaving the retirement accounts outside of the trust, listing their partner as the primary beneficiary, and naming the trust or other individuals as the contingent beneficiaries, the account maintains its tax-deferred status. But what happens if money needs to be taken out when the partner owning the account is incapacitated? The well partner can use the financial power of attorney to access those funds if needed. It is the combination of the partner acting as a trustee of the Domestic Partner AB-SECURE Trust and acting as power of attorney that allows a partner to take control of all finances during a crisis.

Living Will/Advance Directives

The living will may be the simplest document in a legal domestic partner plan, but it may turn out to be the most important one for your partner and loved ones to have. Although the healthcare power of attorney allows your partner and others to make medical decisions for you, the living will takes the final, most difficult decision out of their hands. When it comes to whether or not to administer life support and artificial nutrition and hydration at the end of life, a living will can express your wishes and directions.

Many people remember the Terri Schiavo case from Florida from 2005. In 1990, Terri Schiavo collapsed in her St. Petersburg apartment, and by the time she was rushed to the hospital had suffered severe oxygen deprivation. It soon became clear that she was in a persistent vegetative state, or extremely close to it.

Terri's body was alive, and she did not need to be on ventilators or other mechanical devices. However, she did need to be on feeding tubes and hydration. After several years, her husband finally decided to take her off the feeding tubes and let her pass on naturally. However, Terri's parents interceded and refused to let her go.

What followed was years upon years of court battles. Up and down the court system her case went, with multiple appeals, multiple rulings, and astronomical legal fees paid. Eventually, Congress interceded and took the case out of the Florida state court system and put it into the federal court system, taking a legal step never done before in what was always a state legal matter. Finally, fifteen years after she originally collapsed, Terri had her feeding tubes removed and she passed on.

Whatever your beliefs in this matter may be, the point is the same for all sides—if Terri had only had her wishes in writing, none of the legal battles would have had to take place. Having a living will handles this issue specifically.

Nomination of Conservator

Another important document to have as part of your legal partner plan is a document that nominates your conservator. A conservator is a court appointed guardian. In the event you are unable to handle your own matters, your power of attorney document *should* be all you need to make sure the people you choose handle your healthcare and other matters. However, it is still possible for a judge to stretch his or her authority and start a proceeding to assign you a conservator.

If that happens, it is critical you have a list of conservators in writing *you* prefer. If you have conservators listed, it becomes even harder for a judge to select someone else without a good reason. It is also good practice to make the people you nominated as healthcare power of attorney agents to be the same people nominated as conservators. The jobs are nearly identical, and the criteria for naming a healthcare agent are the same for choosing a conservator. Again, this may be another spare tire, but it is better to have it and not need it than to need it and not have it.

Pour-Over Will

All properly drafted and executed revocable living trusts take the place of the traditional Last Will and Testament, but there is still a need for a document called a Pour-Over Will. In relation to the other documents, it's function is relatively minor. However, it can not be overlooked.

The only true function of a Pour-Over Will is to take assets that may end up in probate and hand them over to the trustee of the revocable living trust to be handled. As you will read in the Chapter on Managing the Trust, title to accounts and other property becomes important. If an asset is titled in the name of the trust, then it will not have to go through the probate process before being distributed to the surviving partner or the other chosen beneficiaries. If it is in the deceased person's name, then it must go through the probate process first. The only way to direct the probate assets to the trust is through the terms of the Pour-Over Will.

While every effort should be made to make sure all possible assets are in the name of the trust or list the trust as a transfer upon death beneficiary of the trust, sometimes there are things that just can not avoid probate. For example, if a partner files their income taxes but passes on before receiving a refund check, then the IRS will only issue a check in the name of that partner's "estate," meaning it has to go through the probate court. Nothing short of timing a death correctly would avoid that problem, and so the Pour-Over Will may be a shadow of a traditional Last Will and Testament, it still may have its uses and should be part of any complete plan.

Nomination of Guardianship

While concepts of child custody and guardian ship could fill an entire book all by themselves, this is not that book. However, a legal partner plan would not be complete without at least having a nomination of guardianship form if you are the parent or guardian of a minor child or incompetent adult. By incompetent, I mean in the legal sense that they are not able to make many of the legal decisions adults can make.

Be sure to also take specific note of the name of the document as it is a "nomination" and not "appointment" of guardian. While laws and rules vary greatly from state to state, there is a general understanding that the guardianship of children and incompetent adults can not be given away like property. While the wishes of a parent or guardian go a long way in a judge making custody decisions after a person passes on, they are by no means conclusive.

When it is seen that many people go years upon years without revising their partner planning documents, a person who was perfectly suitable as a guardian five years before may have become addicted to drugs, been in and out of jail, or even moved halfway around the world. If a person passes on naming a friend or relative who fits that bill, then the need for a judge to make the final decision on who receives guardianship in the best interests of the child (or incompetent adult) is obvious.

While partners would like for there to be an easy path to guaranteeing custody passing to each other, at this time there is no simple solution. But putting those wishes in writing *does* carry a lot of weight, and naming those potential guardians as your partner first, and then backups one at a time and in order, is a necessary part of a legal domestic partner plan.

Assignment of Personal Effects

As we will see in the next chapter, the revocable living trust is only effective if assets are inside the trust or set up to transfer into the trust when someone passes on. An Assignment of Personal Effects form transfers assets that do not have a specific title to them into the name of the trust. For example, furniture, appliances, clothing, and books are all personal effects that are transferred into the trust without changing a title document on each and every individual item.

This is not the case with items such as land and houses, bank accounts, and financial accounts. Those assets have to be retitled, the trust is named as a beneficiary on the account, or some combination of the two. Above all, as you will read in the next chapter, simply having the documents is not enough. Your assets must work in combination with the trust and other documents to take care of you and your partner.

Summary

As you have read in this chapter, a legal domestic partner plan may seem complicated and with a lot of documents, but such a plan is merely complete. Handling the myriad of problems that domestic partners *may* face, whether or not such situations are *likely*, takes planning and foresight. Fortunately, the "big blue binder" with The Estate Plan's Domestic Partner AB-SECURE Trust provides all of the documents referenced in this chapter. To learn more about The Estate Plan's history, please download the free information at http://www.theestateplan.com/files/livingtrusthistory.pdf.

Chapter Eight:
Managing the Plan

We sat at the kitchen table reviewing their father's trust. Mr. John Smith (not his real name) had passed on a week earlier, finally succumbing to cancer. While his children had prepared themselves, Mr. Smith had prepared even more. He had one of the best trusts around, created by a California attorney two years earlier through a company called The Estate Plan. "My father wanted to keep settling things as simple as possible," the daughter said. "That's why he basically liquidated everything and put it into a checking account in the name of the trust."

"That will really make things simple," I said. "As long as all of the medical and other bills are paid, there's no reason not to distribute the funds within the next few weeks. Are you sure that all he had was the one bank account and it was in the name of the trust?"

"Well, yeah," the daughter replied. "Except for these three stocks he wanted to hold on to. They're in his name, not the name of the trust… is that a problem?"

I tried not to sigh too visibly, realizing that while the trust could be settled in the next few weeks, it may be months or up to a year before the stocks were distributed through the probate process.

Once you have a revocable living trust in place for you and your partner, you have to make sure all of your assets work with your trust. In other words, you have to make sure your revocable living trust is funded properly. A revocable living trust will keep all of the assets in the trust from having to go through probate. Therefore, to avoid probate completely, you have to make sure all of your assets are in the trust or are set up to transfer into the trust upon death. Just having the documents is not enough.

Most of the problems people hear about revocable living trusts are just like the stories people hear about hospitals. There is nothing inherently wrong with hospitals. Hospitals and the people who work in them can save your life, help you recover and then release you from their care allowing you to have a longer or better life. But then there are the stories of medication mix-ups, surgeries happening on the wrong person or the wrong part of the body, or a host of other malpractice problems. But all of these problems stem from the practice of medicine being done poorly.

It is the same with a revocable living trust not being effective in doing what it is supposed to do—avoid probate, preserve privacy, lower costs and shorten settlement times. The main area where revocable trusts fall short is when assets are not set up properly to work in conjunction with the trust. And so the revocable living trust naysayers, who are mostly attorneys who do a lot of probate work, are way off target when they suggest people not use revocable trusts at all.

What they should be saying is if you have a revocable living trust, just make sure it is drafted properly and your assets are in place to take full advantage of it. After all, no one is suggesting just because there are mistakes made in hospitals we should simply close them all down—we just need to make sure that things happen the way they are supposed to.

While each asset is a little different, there are three main kinds of changes that have to take place depending on the type of asset. If your revocable living trust was drafted properly and an "assignment of personal assets" or similar form has been used, then all of your personal assets like clothing, furniture and appliances are already in the trust. This even covers things like the food in the refrigerator and the change between the seat cushions. What we need to be concerned with are items such as real estate and timeshares, investment and retirement accounts, bank accounts and other assets that have some sort of title to them.

The first kind of change is re-titling an asset in the name of the revocable living trust. In short, you and your partner are changing these assets so technically you no longer own the asset but your joint trust does. But don't worry. You still control everything in the trust and can still do everything you normally would do as if it were property owned by both of you. The second kind of change is making the trust the primary beneficiary in case you pass on. You still remain the owner on the account, but now when you pass on it can go directly into the trust without having to go through probate to get there. The third change is to make a person the primary beneficiary and the trust becomes the contingent beneficiary. In this instance you keep control of the account, but if you pass it goes to another person, namely your partner, and not the trust. If your partner passes on before you do, then it would go to the trust to be distributed. *The most important thing is that all of these possible transfers happen without probate.*

While there may be different permutations and exceptions, these are the three main kinds of changes that need to be done. We will now go through some specifics on these changes one at a time, discuss which assets require a specific method, and then go into some exceptions, future steps and maintenance. But first, here are a few basics regardless of what kind of change is made.

The Basics

Always use the legal trust name and the legal names of people. The name of the trust is typically found in the first few pages of the revocable living trust. We also prepare a report for our clients called "Property Title and Beneficiary Changes & Designations" and list the proper name of the trust on the first page. This typically reads something like "The Revocable Living Trust of Jessica Tate and Mary Campbell." For a person's name, if their name is John Wilkes Booth or Lee Harvey Oswald, you should not refer to them as Wilkee Booth or Ossie Oswald, even though that is how people generally know them. Always use the full proper name.

One benefit of working with a financial advisor through The Estate Plan is the advisor will outline and assist with a lot of these changes for clients using the exact names and information, and will also work with an attorney for any legal documents needed to make these changes, such as drafting deeds.

Second, always look at what kind of asset or account you are handling and ask "have I paid income taxes on this yet?" This is actually a big consideration. Any account that is "tax-qualified," meaning it is for retirement and you were able to put that money away without paying income taxes on it, should never be transferred directly into the name of the trust. If you do, then IRS regulations may treat that as if you had taken all of the money out in one year, and you are subject to taxes and possibly penalties. If you are in doubt, contact your attorney or tax professional before making any such change.

Finally, start with a list of all of your accounts and assets that have some kind of title to them and make sure you go through the list until all of the changes are completed.

Re-titling assets in the name of the trust

In some cases, re-titling an asset so it is in the name of the trust is the best course of action. This is certainly the case with real estate, and is best for mutual funds, savings accounts, checking accounts, money market accounts, and other non-qualified brokerage accounts. By non-qualified, I mean that you have paid income taxes on the money before you put it into the account. As a word of caution, unless you are working with a financial advisor affiliated with The Estate Plan we encourage people to handle as many of the transfers on their own as they can to save on the costs of funding the trust. However, transferring ownership of real estate and timeshares involves preparing a legal deed to make those transfers. Drafting a deed is something only a licensed attorney should do, so if this has not been taken care of by your attorney, contact him or her.

In making changes to accounts, the type of form you would need is probably titled something like a "change of ownership" or "change of title." In any event, your financial advisor or personnel at the institution should know which form is required to change the ownership of the account in the right way. If your advisor does not know, contact your attorney and have him or her speak with the financial institution.

Changing the primary beneficiary

There are also some situations where changing the ownership is not as beneficial as changing the beneficiary. The best example is a life insurance policy. The most important part of the life insurance contract is who gets the proceeds. In this case, the trust is the right beneficiary. While it is possible to make the revocable living trust the owner, the paperwork is usually much more involved and has no added benefit. Instead, it becomes easier to keep your life insurance policy in your name and simply make your trust the primary beneficiary. Upon death, all it would take is a copy of the death certificate for the proceeds to pay into your trust.

Please also note at this point we are talking about situations that don't involve estate tax problems. If you have large life insurance policies and may be subject to estate taxes, other steps can be taken to account for ownership of life insurance while saving estate taxes through an Irrevocable Life Insurance Trust.

Changing the contingent beneficiary

Finally, there are a few situations where you want to keep ownership of an account, name another individual as the primary beneficiary, and then list the trust as the contingent or secondary beneficiary. In all of these cases, you are naming a spouse or partner the primary beneficiary of an IRA, 401K or other tax-qualified account for income tax purposes, and then listing your living trust as the contingent beneficiary. For married couples, there are special benefits regarding tax-qualified accounts in that the surviving spouse can do a "roll-over" when one spouse passes on, meaning placing the assets in the account into the spouse's own IRA and then take the money out when he or she chooses. In doing so, there can be some considerable tax-deferred growth, but the main catch is this is only available to spouses right now.

We also recommend this same set up be done for tax-qualified accounts for domestic partners even though they are not married. Our reason for making this recommendation is the funds are still going to the person they want, and if that person passes on first, it will still end up in the trust to be distributed to other beneficiaries when the second partner passes on. Under some new federal laws, domestic partners have the opportunity to defer income taxes when they inherit their partner's retirement account. (For more information, please download the free report at www.domesticpartneriras.com) Also, if in the future domestic partners gain the same "roll-over" option, the accounts will already be set up properly and another change will not be necessary. But until that time, there is nothing lost in still setting up the beneficiaries on the accounts this way.

Difficult items

And now, because we are not in a perfect world, there are a few items that present difficulties. First and foremost, there are automobiles. The main problem with handling automobiles, at least in North Carolina, is that auto insurance agents generally don't understand what we are doing in setting up a revocable living trust, and so they feel compelled to say your car is now a corporate vehicle, therefore the coverage is much higher and your premiums will go up. There is also no way to put a transfer upon death beneficiary designation on a car title, and therefore there is no way to have the automobiles avoid probate without creating hassles during life. But as I tell my clients, as long as your trustee has the car keys and the car is registered and insured, it really doesn't matter if it takes a few months for the car to go through probate.

The second item that creates some difficulties is CDs. Certificates of Deposit are typically registered in the owner's name and can't be changed until the certificates become due without having substantial penalties. Therefore, the advice our firm typically gives is to wait until the CDs are due, and then if you wish to keep the proceeds invested in CDs, work with the bank to re-title them in the name of the trust at that time. Also, it may be worth checking with the bank to see if it can somehow place a beneficiary designation on the CD. Then it is probably easier to simply list the trust as the primary beneficiary.

Finally, while this is not really a difficult step in initially funding the trust, a lot of my clients have had some difficulty in refinancing a mortgage once the land is in the trust. The fact is despite the large increase in the use of revocable living trusts over the past 20 years and more, a lot of mortgage lenders still panic when they see the property is in a trust. *Don't let their panic affect you.* Typically all that is needed is a few pages of the trust faxed to the lender, or in some rare cases, a letter from the attorney. If your lender is still in a panic or requires you to transfer your property back into your name before it will refinance, then it may be time to consider another mortgage lender. If not, then one deed must be created and executed transferring the land back into your individual name, and then a second deed should be executed after the refinancing is completed in order to transfer the property back into the trust.

We have gone over all of the different kinds of transfers, the different kinds of assets, what needs to be done to each, and even reviewed some trouble areas. If everything is done properly, your revocable living trust should now be complete and well-funded. But what happens next? As you go forward in life, there will be many opportunities to open new accounts, buy and sell properties, and make transfers. Each time you have a new asset with a title or account name on it, something needs to be done to make sure it works with the trust. In these cases, simply review this program again to see what needs to be done.

As a word of caution again about mortgages, if you are buying property in the future and will have a mortgage on it, it may be more convenient, and certainly less stressful, to initially purchase the property in your own name, wait about two weeks, and then transfer the property into the name of the trust. In general, this just makes things run more smoothly.

With most situations in this book, we recommend you consult with an attorney who fully understands legal partner planning. However, with regard to funding your trust, you will receive even better help with a financial advisor who understands the same field. The Estate Plan has a nationwide network of such advisors who typically work with estate planning attorneys. As I have also mentioned, my firm is available to consult with all advisors and attorneys who are in The Estate Plan's network, and certified professionals can be found through The National Institute for Domestic Partner Estate Planning.

Summary

The right revocable living trust can provide domestic partners with many of benefits they are looking for, but the trust only works if it is properly funded. In general, assets have to be re-titled in the name of the trust, set up so the account pays into the trust upon death, or set up so the account pays out first to the partner and second to the trust. For more information on funding a revocable living trust, check out the podcast on this subject, available in the Resources section of www.gaymarriagealternative.com. For specific information and legal advice, contact an attorney in your state or jurisdiction.

Chapter Nine: The National Institute For Domestic Partner Estate Planning, The Estate Plan™ and Other Resources

Wow, the pasta looked good. Don and Frank had been going to their church's annual potluck fundraiser for four years now, and their neighbor Charlie's pasta seemed to get better each year. Thankfully, Don and Frank were able to find a progressive church that not only didn't discriminate against them but welcomed them.

"So, when is the big day?" Agnes asked.

While Agnes was a friend, she was also in charge of the church bulletin and liked to get information as far in advance as possible. Of course, she was referring to their upcoming commitment ceremony. Don's mouth was full of pasta, so Frank answered her instead. "Three months from tomorrow," he answered

"Do you have everything in order?" Charlie the master chef asked, joining in the conversation.

"Just about," Don was able to answer. "We have the reception location booked, the caterer booked, most of the details are in place, and the invites go out next week."

"Have you taken care of your legal documents?" Charlie asked. While Charlie loved to cook, he was also a wealth of information on all things gay ever since his brother Everett came out a decade ago and brought his partner to Thanksgiving dinner. Since then, Charlie did the research to help his brother and partner not make any mistakes.

Frank and Don looked at each other. "Not yet," Don said. "I thought we'd go through the Yellow Pages after the honeymoon and find an attorney to help out."

Charlie frowned. "I have a better idea," he said. "When my brother and his partner got their papers in order, I did a lot of research."

Of course.

"While Everett and Michael have revised their plans over the years, I found information on the Web about a national organization that focuses specifically on estate planning for domestic partners," Charlie said. "The National Institute for Domestic Partner Estate Planning had a list of attorneys and other professionals who were able to set them up with the best documents available. I can send you the link."

Don and Frank looked at each other, and Don raised his eyebrow. "Great pasta and great advice… how can we go wrong?"

One of the most critical starting points in domestic partners putting together an effective, comprehensive domestic partner plan is finding the right professionals to work with. Because of the complexity, problem areas, and, yes, the stigma some professionals place on working with domestic partners, there has been a shortage of help for LGBT couples. Thankfully, there are a growing number of attorneys, accountants and financial advisors gaining knowledge in this area through The National Institute for Domestic Partner Estate Planning (www.NIDPestateplanning.com). And thanks to The Estate Plan™ offering The Domestic Partner AB-SECURE Trust™, an excellent solution in reaching domestic partner planning goals is available nationwide through all professionals affiliated with The Estate Plan™ (www.theestateplan.com).

The National Institute for Domestic Partner Estate Planning

Founded in 2008, the Institute has since focused on providing extensive information and ongoing training to attorneys, financial advisors, and accountants in helping their domestic partner clients create and maintain effective partner plans. In addition, the Institute only offers membership to professionals who have received proper education and have passed stringent ethical background checks.

Because it is difficult enough to find a domestic partner planning professional who understands domestic partner planning, and it is nerve-wracking enough searching for an LGBT-friendly attorney or other professional, The National Institute for Domestic Partner Estate Planning has created rigorous membership requirements. Therefore, you can feel confident that the professionals who are members of the Institute understand the traps and minefields to be avoided and how to properly apply effective solutions in domestic partners reaching their goals.

Each member must:

1) Attend a basic life and estate planning training session planned and coordinated by The Abts Institute for Estate Preservation and pass a test (or have similar basic estate planning training approved by the Institute)
2) Attend a two-day specialized legal domestic partner planning training session planned and coordinated by The National Institute for Domestic Partner Estate Planning, LLC and taught by Jeffrey G. Marsocci, author of *Estate Planning for Domestic Partners*, and pass an exam
3) Pass an extensive professional background check and be admitted as a member of the National Ethics Bureau.
4) Pass a re-accreditation exam every two years

The basic training provided by The Estate Plan™ was originally developed by Henry W. Abts III, author of *The Living Trust*, and has been updated over the years to provide the most current basic estate planning information available. All attorneys, accountants and financial advisors affiliated with The Estate Plan™ have this course available to them. At the time of this printing, the Institute is waiving the basic course for applicants with significant experience and holding accredited designations such as Certified Estate Planner (CEP) from The National Institute of Certified Estate Planners. People holding these designations have typically shown proven competence in the basic life and estate planning processes and documents.

The intensive, two-day course held by the Institute is mandatory and all members of The National Institute for Domestic Partner Estate Planning have also passed a stringent exam displaying true knowledge of the legal domestic partner planning arena. (One member of the inaugural class remarked that the exam was the most difficult they had taken since taking their professional boards.)

Rather than taking on the tasks of running background and licensing checks, the Institute has taken advantage of the services provided by The National Ethics Bureau. The National Ethics Bureau requires professional, ethical and criminal background checks prior to admittance to membership, and therefore the Institute requires membership of all accountants and financial advisors. It is expected that attorneys will also be offered membership in the National Ethics Bureau in the near future.

Finally, as benefits of membership the Institute provides ongoing education and information to its members, and an exam must be passed every two years in order to maintain membership. Therefore, professionals who are on the Institute's membership roll have not only received extensive training initially, they have also passed exams every two years to maintain their membership.

The professionals who have become members of the Institute are the best and brightest, and they have gained the necessary background to help domestic partners create and maintain an effective partner plan.

The Estate Plan™

When initially putting together *Estate Planning for Domestic Partners: The Legal Secrets You Need to Know to Protect Your Partner and Your Future* (www.estateplanningfordomesticpartners.com), it was decided that a practical trust solution had to be available nationwide. Without a readily available solution to help domestic partners reach their goals, the only thing a book would do is point out the failings in the legal community to address the needs of LGBT couples. Therefore, in conjunction with The Estate Plan™, a trust was created that would be available in all 50 states.

And so The Domestic Partner AB-SECURE Trust™ was born. All professionals affiliated with The Estate Plan™ have access to this trust, the accompanying Domestic Partnership Property Agreement, and the ancillary documents mentioned in this book, in one package. By teaming up with a prestigious trust education and document production company with more than 25 years in operation, members of the National Institute for Domestic Partner Estate Planning have a readily available, customizable set of documents to help domestic partners achieve their goals.

In addition to The Domestic Partner AB-SECURE Trust™, The Estate Plan™ also carries a wide array of specialized trusts for different tax and personal situations. For more information on other solutions provided by The Estate Plan™, please contact them directly at 1-800-350-1234.

Other Resources

While it is critical for domestic partners to put together the right legal partner plan to reach their goals, not all of their goals are met through document planning. Income taxes intrude on everyone's lives, and paying the least amount legally permissible is a goal everyone except the government can embrace, but it is not really *legal* partner planning. Owning a house the correct way and providing for its inheritance is an integral part of many domestic partners' *legal* partner plan, but the purchase, mortgage, and maintenance of a home is beyond the scope of *legal documents* portion of partner planning.

While not fully a part of life and estate planning, there are resources to help with these and other areas of interest for domestic partners available at www.gaymarriagealternative.com. At this site, you can find:

- Free downloadable reports
- Audio programs for sale by download or on CD
- Books for sale in e-book format or paperback
- Links to other sites of interest

There are an abundance of tools and resources available at this website for domestic partners, and they are not limited to the life and estate planning arena. Since the law does not automatically protect domestic partners, a little research before making major life decisions can yield tremendous benefits or avoid disastrous mistakes.

Summary

While there are specific recommended documents for domestic partners which can help reach their life and estate planning goals, it is also highly recommended that domestic partners work with professionals skilled in helping LGBT couples. They can be found at The National Institute for Domestic Partner Estate Planning at www.NIDPestateplanning.com.

In addition, life and estate planning documents for domestic partners should be the best available and capable of being customized for each partner's specific desires and needs. To help attorneys and other professionals meet these needs, The Estate Plan™ now offers its affiliated attorneys, accountants and financial advisors The Domestic Partner AB-SECURE Trust™ with accompanying Domestic Partnership Property Agreement.

Finally, domestic partner planning is not completely about estate planning. However, an abundance of resources for domestic partners can be found at www.gaymarriagealternative.com to provide critical information before taking legal, financial or life decisions.

With the law stacked against domestic partners, having the right information before making critical decisions can help you navigate legal pitfalls and take advantage of the private, legal solutions that are available… under the current law and without having to enact gay marriage in your state.

Appendix A:
Members of The National Institute for Domestic Partner Estate Planning

Below are the members of The National Institute for Domestic Partner Estate Planning as of April 20, 2009. New members will be inducted approximately 3 times per year after attending their certification training and passing their exam. In order by admittance class:

Founder, 2008

Jeffrey G. Marsocci, Attorney
8406 Six Forks Road, Suite 102
Raleigh, North Carolina 27615
(919) 844-7993
nclawyer@earthlink.net
www.theestategeek.com

Certified October 2008

Roberta Hall, Reno, Nevada

Robertahall7@yahoo.com

Geri McHam, The Estate Plan, Reno, Nevada

GeriMcHam@theestateplan.com

W. Larry Sherman, Financial Advisor
1211 West 5th Street
Laurel, Mississippi 39440
(601) 425-3707
shermanpa@bellsouth.net

Sue Stringer, Financial Advisor
1020 Steven Drive
Alvin, Texas 77511
(281) 796-0770
sstringer@tarkentonfinancial.com

Bette Wagner
1845 Country Road 1400 NW
Urbana, Illinois 61802
(271) 621-9049
bette@wagnerestateplanning.com

Certified February 2009

Mary Ann Andrews, Financial Advisor
68 Calle Enrique
Santa Fe, New Mexico 87507
(505) 699-3080
Maandrews6849@gmail.com

Glen Pier, Financial Advisor
3400 Sweeten Creek Road, Suite A
Arden, North Carolina 28704
(828) 681-8574
glenpier@infinityretirement.com

As more professionals are certified and admitted as members of The National Institute for Domestic Partner Estate Planning, this list will be updated in the e-book versions and new members will also be added to the physical book as new copies are printed and placed into inventory. For the most up to date information on members, please visit the Institute at www.NIDPestateplanning.com.

Appendix B:
5 Questions to Ask Professionals About Partner Protection Planning

Choosing a professional to assist you with your partner protection planning documents can be one of the most important decisions you and your partner can make. Having the wrong documents can create confusion, added expenses, and cause delays in a time of crisis. The worst part is believing you and your partner are protected and not realizing you were wrong until it is too late to do anything about it. By finding the right professional the first time to assist you with creating a comprehensive, effective partner protection plan that helps you both reach your goals, you can avoid the chaos. Instead when your documents are needed most, you will find things ordered, efficient, and administratively inexpensive. Here are five questions to ask your attorney or other professional *before* getting your documents done.

On the following pages are the five questions to ask professionals when interviewing them about Partner Protection Planning and the differing answers you are likely to receive. At the end of the five questions is a scoring sheet to assist you in making a decision about working with a professional or not. Please keep in mind that these are guidelines, and you should always use your own best judgment in finding the right professionals to work with you.

1. Do you generally recommend or discuss Wills, Separate Revocable Living Trusts, or a Joint Revocable Living Trust for domestic partners?

_______ Wills (0). Except for doing nothing, this is the worst answer, especially if the professional follows it up with "you don't have enough assets to warrant use of a trust." This shows that they are either woefully ignorant of the problems partners can face during the probate process, or they figure they can make a lot more money helping with the bureaucratic tsunami known as probate later. Either is unacceptable. Take off an additional 5 points if they argue "the probate fees in our state are not that high." What they are saying is that court costs are not high, but what they charge to handle probate paperwork probably is.

_______ Separate Revocable Living Trusts (15). At least they are on the right track by understanding that you can not simply lump assets together without violating the gift tax rules, but they are not really giving partners the best plan they could.

_______ A Joint Revocable Living Trust (20). If they simply say use a joint revocable living trust and nothing more, ask about the gift tax. If they mention the Domestic Partnership Property Agreement or some sort of "separate property agreement," then give full credit. If they stare at you blankly or have no idea what you are talking about, only give 5 points instead of 20.

2. What courses or instruction have you received in estate planning in general and partner planning in particular?

_______ Nothing or little (0). If the attorney or other professional only attends continuing education courses in estate planning every few years, then give them the opportunity to discuss the courses they have had and any independent research they may have made. If you have read *Estate Planning for Domestic Partners* or *The Gay Marriage Alternative* and know more than they do about partner planning, then they definitely deserve 0 points.

_______ Some or a lot of general estate planning, but not as much in partner planning (10 points). An attorney or other professional who understands general estate planning principals and keeps extremely up to date, at least twice a year, but does not receive any education in partner planning is still not going to be a good professional for domestic partners. Ask about their own independent research and be forgiving in granting the 10 points if they have done some research into the area. Aside from training from The National Institute for Domestic Partner Estate Planning, there is very little training on partner planning available.

_______ A lot of general and partner planning specific education and training (20 points). If the professional attends at least three courses per year in estate planning and at least two courses per year for partner planning, then they are making strong efforts to obtain the right information and training. If they are a member of The National Institute for Domestic Partner Estate Planning, then they attend partner planning educational phone calls each quarter. Give an additional 5 points if the professional teaches general estate planning classes to other professionals *or* give an additional 10 points if they specifically teach partner planning to other professionals.

3. How should our accounts and home be titled?

_______ Joint with a right of survivorship (0 points). If the professional simply says their assets should be titled as joint with a right of survivorship and does not mention anything about gift tax forms, then they clearly do not understand the ramifications of the federal gift tax.

_______ Keep them the way they are because of the gift tax (5 points). At least the professional understands there is a gift tax, which puts them ahead of many other professionals who would jump to joint property as a solution. However, simply doing nothing offers no solutions at all.

_______ Joint with a right of survivorship, but gift tax forms or a property agreement may be necessary (15 points). At least with the additional agreements or filing of gift tax forms, the professional understands the gift tax is a problem and they are offering some kind of solution. It is not the optimal solution, but with a little additional information, they can probably handle partner planning fairly effectively.

_______ Retitle in name of a joint trust but only with a Domestic Partnership Property Agreement (20 points). Here the professional is showing that they understand the problems with the gift tax, but they have suggested the optimal solution of avoiding probate, providing joint control, and avoiding the federal gift tax.

4. When domestic partners come to you after trying to do partner planning on their own and they feel they messed something up, what do you usually see? (Please choose the *closest* answer.)

_______ We don't have many domestic partner clients, but we usually correct their planning mistakes by setting up the same documents we use for married couples. Basically, it's the same thing. (0 points). This is tap dancing on the part of the professional, and they are mixing up the desire to treat clients equally with the fact that domestic partner planning is different. Sorry, no points for good intentions.

_______ Usually the mistakes we see are partners who retiled their assets as joint with a right of survivorship. We usually separate the assets out and use Wills for correct partner planning. (5 points.) Here they are undoing the problem, hopefully, but not offering a better solution at all for avoiding probate.

_______ Usually the mistakes we see are partners who retiled their assets as joint with a right of survivorship. We separate the assets and use separate living trusts for correct partner planning. (15 points.) Here they are undoing the problem, and providing a means to avoid probate, but they are not making the plan the best it could be.

_______ There are usually a variety of mistakes we see from partners, including triggering the gift tax through joint property with a right of survivorship, and other problems with documents being inadequate. Usually we separate the assets out, form a joint trust with a separate property agreement, and then retitle the accounts in the name of the trust while avoiding the gift tax through the separate property agreement. (20 points). This is really the best of all possible worlds going forward. It avoids probate, gives joint control, and avoids future gift tax problems.

5. What precautions can we put in place to make sure my partner is calling the shots if I become ill?

_______ "There isn't anything you have to do" or "there isn't anything you can do." (0 points). If you get either answer, then run far and run fast. The only exception is in marriage equality states there may be some laws that empower partners to handle things as the spouse. In that case, still give them zero points because they were assuming that you would never leave the state. The fact is if you travel to a state that does not recognize gay marriage, they will likely deny you the right to make medical and financial decisions for each other.

_______ "We should set you up with a healthcare power of attorney and a durable power of attorney, and that will take care of everything." (10 points). They have the basic documents used to empower each other during life, but sometimes financial institutions insist on *their* in-house form being used. During a time of crisis, delays and denials because of "incorrect forms" are no comfort.

_______ "While we should use a healthcare power of attorney and a durable power of attorney, having your own revocable living trusts and naming each other as a co-trustees can provide a more seamless transition if one of you become sick." (15 points). They clearly understand the basic principles around partner planning, but it is still not the most effective way to handle things.

_______ "While we should use a healthcare power of attorney and a durable power of attorney, you should have a joint revocable living trust with a separate property agreement, and both of you are full trustees. This can provide a more seamless transition if one of you become sick." (20 points). They clearly understand partner protection planning, and they realize that one joint trust becomes easier to administer in a time of crisis.

Scoring:

75-100+	The professional clearly understands the principles surrounding partner protection planning, and using their services are likely to get you and your partner the maximum planning effectiveness available under the law.
60-74	All things considered, they are probably ahead of other attorneys and professionals, but they are not the best choice. However, they show promise and if they are willing to review *Estate Planning for Domestic Partners* or consider going through the training with The National Institute for Domestic Partner Estate Planning, then they may be worth pursuing… especially if there are no other professionals within your area.
50-59	A borderline walk-out. Without a strong willingness on their part to learn more about partner protection planning and get up to speed, it is time to leave.
49 or lower	They clearly are not suited for giving you effective partner protection planning documents and services. Thank them for their time and leave.

As an added note, while the most important goal for you may be gaining the best partner protection planning documents available, professionals in the 60-74 point range above are still worth considering if they are willing to learn the principles behind the planning. You have to also be comfortable with the professionals you work with, so a professional you like with a good understanding of the basics who is willing to learn may be a better fit for you and your partner than a professional with higher scores whom you simply do not get along with. And remember that these questions are not legal advice but merely information to help you in choosing the right advisors. Please keep this in mind when choosing the right professional *for you.*

Made in the USA
Las Vegas, NV
17 April 2026

45526409R00073